The Marshall Cavendish

International
WILDLIFE
ENCYCLOPEDIA

VOLUME 6
COC – CRO

MARSHALL CAVENDISH

NEW YORK · LONDON · TORONTO · SYDNEY

Introduction by: Professor D.L. Aller
General Editors: Dr Maurice Burton and Robert Burton
Consultant Editor: Mark Lambert
Production: Brenda Glover
Design: Eric Rose
Editorial Director: Nicolas Wright

Revised Edition Published 1990

Published by Marshall Cavendish Corporation
147 West Merrick Road
Freeport, Long Island
N.Y. 11520

Managing Editor: Mark Dartford BA
Editor: Nigel Rodgers MA
Production: Robert Paulley BA
Design: Edward Pitcher

Printed and bound in Italy by LEGO Spa Vicenza

Library of Congress Cataloging-in-Publication Data

Marshall Cavendish International wildlife encyclopedia/general
  editors, Maurice Burton and Robert Burton.
    p. cm.
    ''Portions of this work have also been published as The
International wildlife encyclopedia, Encyclopedia of animal life and
Funk & Wagnalls wildlife encyclopedia.''
    Includes index.
    Contents: v. 6. COC-CRO.
    ISBN 0-86307-734-X (set).
    ISBN 0-86307-740-4 (v. 6).
    1. Zoology–Collected works. I. Burton, Maurice, 1898-
II. Burton, Robert, 1941-   . III. Title: International wildlife
encyclopedia.
QL3.M35 1988
591'.03'21–dc 19

Volume 6

Cockatoo

Cockatoos have crests which they can erect at will, distinguishing the 16 species from the rest of the parrot family. Most cockatoos are white, sometimes with pink or yellow tinges and coloured crests. Some are black, such as the great palm or black cockatoo, which is all black, except for a bare patch of pink on the cheeks that blushes red if the cockatoo is angry or excited, or turns blue if it is unwell. Another, the gang-gang, has a dark grey body with a scarlet crest like a lady's toque, and the galah or rose-breasted cockatoo has a grey back and underwings and a rosy breast. Flocks of galahs make an impressive sight as they wheel about, flashing grey and pink alternately. The corella used to have the apt but descriptive name of 'the bloodstained cockatoo'.

The best known of the cockatoos, common as cage birds, are the white or sulphur-crested cockatoo, and the hardy and easily bred cockatiel, crested parrot, or quarrion Nymphicus hollandicus, *that was at one time classed outside the cockatoos. The name cockatoo is derived from their call.*

Raucous flocks

Cockatoos are found in the Australasian region from the Celebes in the west to the Solomon Islands in the east. They are birds of wooded country but some are found more in the open. The cockatiel, for instance, is found in woodland bordering rivers or in open scrub of the Australian interior. It is a nomad, living in flocks of up to several thousand that roam the country, settling where food and water are plentiful.

Although it feeds in the open, the cockatiel retires to the woods or forests to roost at night, as does the great palm cockatoo. The latter sleeps alone, each bird having a roost on a high, preferably bare branch. Unlike most other birds, the great palm cockatoos do not leave their roost until the sun is quite high. They then congregate in one tree and display, raising their crests and bowing to each other with wings extended and tails raised. As more cockatoos join the gathering the displays become more intense and the birds more excited. Each bow is accompanied by a loud call of two notes, the second being shrill and drawn out. Eventually the noisy party sets out to feed, returning to shelter from the midday heat and finally retiring at nightfall.

While the flock is feeding, a sentinel is posted on a nearby tree, ready to give the alarm if an enemy approaches. When it feels that it has done its fair share, the sentinel flies down to the flock and pecks another cockatoo, who then takes over.

Unfortunately cockatoos are pests of agriculture. The cockatiel, for instance, is a

John Tashiian at San Diego Zoo

Symbol of alarm: great palm or black cockatoo with its crest at battle stations.

pest of sorghum, a cereal crop. As a result some of these colourful and attractive birds are now very much reduced in numbers, but others still abound in large flocks, to the disgust of some farmers, and the galah has actually spread, because man's agricultural activities provide suitable habitats.

Good talkers

There has also been some hunting of the wild cockatoo populations because of their popularity as cage birds. Except in rare species, however, trapping cockatoos is unlikely to have any effect on numbers. Apart from their colourful plumage, cockatoos are popular for their mimicking abilities and intelligence. Like other members of the parrot family they can learn a wide range of human words, animal noises such as the clucking of hens and barks of dogs, as well as mechanical sounds. They can also learn tricks such as bowing and shaking hands. Some species, however, have the disadvantage of having an ear-splitting screech that makes them highly unsuitable as indoor pets.

Nutcrackers

Cockatoos are mainly vegetarian, eating seeds, fruits and nuts. The corella has an unusually long beak, apparently used to dig out roots. Cockatoos that feed on the ground where they can find the seeds of grasses and herbs are the main pests, because cereal crops form a good source of food to hungry flocks, which trample the plants as well as take the seeds. Other cockatoos attack apples and other fruit which they tear apart to get the seeds. Some, however, do some good, as they eat plants that cause paralysis and blindness in domestic animals. The black cockatoos of Australia break off twigs of mulga and other plants, apparently for no other reason than amusement. During droughts the leaves of these scrub plants are an important food supply for sheep, who follow the cockatoos to strip the twigs that have been snapped off and are lying on the ground. Gang-gangs have also been seen cutting off eucalyptus twigs apparently 'just for fun', and also feeding on the insects in eucalyptus galls.

The great palm cockatoo feeds on grubs it finds by tearing open rotten wood, as well as seeds and fruit. It has also made a name for itself by feeding on the thick-shelled fruit of certain palms. Observers who have watched the cockatoos opening them with their powerful bills have described how several blows with an axe are needed to crack the shell. It is not for nothing that visitors to zoos are warned not to poke their fingers through the bars of a cockatoo's cage.

Air-conditioned nests?

Some cockatoos, such as the corella and the galah, breed in colonies, others, such as the yellow-black cockatoo, nest alone. Their nests are in hollows in trees, or in holes in cliffs, and the corellas sometimes use holes in termite mounds. The hollow is lined with leaves or wood chips on which the eggs, usually 4 or 5 in number, are laid. Galahs sometimes strip the bark off the nesting tree to make a ring of smooth wood below the nest hole. This might have the effect of preventing egg-eating lizards from climbing

Eye-catching plumage, nutcracker beak: the rose-breasted cockatoo. Left: Sulphur-crested cockatoo.

up to the nest.

The eggs are incubated for about a month by both sexes and the babies fed in the nest hole until fledged. The cockatiel has been reported to wet its feathers in a nearby pool or river before entering the nest for a spell of incubation. Presumably this helps to keep the air in the nest moist and cool during the heat of the day.

Exotic friends

It is not unusual for cage birds to escape or even to be released deliberately. In some cases this has led to an exotic bird becoming established, perhaps as a pest. Bulbuls have become established in many places (see page 433), but the British Isles are too cold for exotic cage birds to breed in freedom, although they can survive for a while. Reports are continually being made of birds that defy identification from ordinary bird books, and these usually turn out to be 'escapes' from aviaries.

One such was a sulphur-crested cockatoo that lived on Wimbledon Common, in South London. The cockatoo teamed up with three rooks who became its constant companions. This is not surprising as cockatoos live in flocks and rooks, which also live in flocks, would seem to be a suitable choice. Other members of the parrot family have also been seen with British birds. An African grey parrot lived for some years in a rookery in South London, apparently on good terms with its hosts, and there are several records of budgerigars having escaped from the cages of their owners and later joining flocks of sparrows.

class	**Aves**		
order	**Psittaciformes**		
family	**Psittacidae**		
genera & species	***Probosciger aterrimus*** *great palm cockatoo* ***Eolophus roseicapilla*** *galah* ***Cacatua sanguinea*** *corella* ***C. galerita*** *sulphur-crested cockatoo others.*		

Cockchafer

A large beetle, also known as the May bug, which is seen and heard flying about on summer evenings. It is a member of the scarab family and related to the dor beetles and dung beetles. Nearly 1 in. long, it is a very 'square' beetle with a broad and deep abdomen. The elytra, or wing cases, are reddish-brown and do not cover the whole of the abdomen. A conical 'tail' protrudes from under them. The head and thorax are black, and under the body there is a dense layer of hair-like bristles. A feature of the chafers and their relatives is the elaborate antennae, which end in a fan of thin plates. These structures give rise to the name Lamellicornia, or leaf-horns, for a superfamily of beetles, as the fan resembles the leaves of a half-opened book.

Many beetles of this family are known as chafers, a name derived from the Anglo-Saxon for beetle. In the British Isles, there is the garden chafer, or June bug, with green head and thorax and a dark yellowish red abdomen. The rose chafer has a bright golden green and white-spotted abdomen with copper underside and black legs and antennae—an attractive combination when found among the petals of a rose. In North America, other chafers, especially noticed because they bang into lighted windows or strike motor-car windscreens are called May bugs and June bugs. In Assam there lives the giant cockchafer, 3 in. long with front legs of over $2\frac{1}{2}$ in. Each leg has two sharp spurs.

Pests as adults . . .

Both larval and adult chafers damage plants. The larvae attack the roots while the adults eat the leaves and petals or suck sap and nectar. They are called May or June bugs because, although the adults emerge from pupation about October, they do not start to fly until early summer but may be as early as April. Cockchafers can then be seen in large numbers on fine evenings as the light is fading, sometimes climbing up grass stalks and vigorously pumping their abdomens in and out, presumably to warm the body before takeoff, in the same way as an athlete warms up before a race. They then fly off through the grass with the same ponderous, meandering flight as a bumble bee, and also producing a humming noise with the very rapid wingbeats, although the wingbeat of the cockchafer is slow, 46 beats/second, compared with 130–240, that of bumble bees. At other times they can be seen flying around trees such as oaks or flowering chestnuts.

The adults feed on the foliage of trees, and when abundant can cause serious damage by stripping all the leaves. The rose chafer, a day-flyer, lives on the petals of flowers, especially roses. The giant chafer feeds on nectar.

. . . and as larvae

The females lay several batches of eggs in the early summer. Each batch numbers a dozen to 30, totalling about 70. The eggs are laid in burrows 6–8 in. deep, and hatch in 3 weeks. The larva is familiar to anyone who has dug the garden as a large white grub with a brown head and three pairs of legs very near the head.

The larvae of some chafers live in rotten trees and logs through which they burrow, grinding up the wood with their strong, horny jaws and digesting it with the help of bacteria in the gut that can break down cellulose, the main constituent of wood. They are probably important in helping the breakdown and conversion into humus of dead trees, but they also cause considerable damage in timber plantations. The larvae of the rose chafer also live in dead trees, and because these are no longer

△ *Cockchafers mating. The female lays several batches of eggs, totalling about 70.*

▷ *A cockchafer drones in for a landing on young leaves. Large numbers of chafers can cause much damage to trees by stripping them of foliage.*

Joyce Pope

Klaus Meier-Ude : Bavaria

△ *Cockchafer larva. Armed with powerful jaws, they spend 3 years in the soil before pupating.*

△ *Breaking surface: a cockchafer digs its way out after pupating. This happens about October.*

▽ *Truffles grow beneath the soil, but one type of chafer can smell them out as it flies.*

▽ *Complex fan antennae make for sensitivity, and the chafer uses them to seek food.*

tolerated in highly efficient agricultural areas, the rose chafer is becoming less common.

The larva of the cockchafer spends 3 years in the soil before pupating, but this period depends on the climate. Each winter it burrows down, avoiding the frost, and returns to the surface in spring to feed on roots of grass, wheat and other plants including trees, often causing great damage. At the end of their third summer the larvae burrow down and pupate in a cocoon some 2 or 3 ft beneath the surface, emerging as adults a few months later. The larvae are sometimes called white grubs or rookworms, rooks being a particular enemy.

Careful enemy

The manner in which a rook deals with the grub is of special interest. It holds the grub under one foot and bites off the head so getting rid of the grub's strong jaws. Next, the bird pulls off the spiky legs and discards these also. Then it squeezes the soft body with its bill, eats the semi-liquid contents that ooze and finally discards the tough skin.

Truffle hunters

Antennae are sensory organs, reacting to airborne vibrations and to chemicals or, in plain language, to sound and smell. By examining an insect's antennae we can easily see whether it has great or small powers of hearing or smell. If the antennae are well-developed, then the chances are that the insect is highly sensitive. For instance, we find that male mosquitoes have well developed antennae but females have only small ones, and experiments have shown that male mosquitoes' antennae are 'tuned in' to the hum of the female's wingbeats. In this way the sexes are drawn together for mating. The chafers also have elaborate antennae, the fan being spread out when it is in use, but they are well developed in both sexes, so it would seem that their main use is not as a device to lead the males to the females. Both sexes must make use of their antennae, and it seems they are used for finding food.

There is one chafer that feeds on truffles, which are fungi that grow under the surface of the soil. The chafer will suddenly stop in flight, drop to the ground and dig down to where a truffle is buried.

To be able to scent something buried in the ground is, to us, a remarkable achievement, but many animals feed on truffles including squirrels, mice, badgers and deer. Truffles are also esteemed by gourmets and in various parts of Europe, including southern England, dogs, especially poodles, and pigs have been used to hunt them.

phylum	**Arthopoda**
class	**Insecta**
order	**Coleoptera**
family	**Scarabaeidae**
genera & species	***Melolontha melolontha*** cockchafer ***Phyllopertha horticola*** *garden chafer* ***Cetonia floricola*** *rose chafer* *others*

Cockle

Of the various cockles of British coasts, the commonest by far is the edible cockle. Although its scientific name is now Cerastoderma edule, it is referred to in many books by the older name of Cardium edule, a name that reflects the heart-shaped appearance of the pair of shells viewed end-on, as well as the tastiness of their contents. The cockle is an unusually globular bivalve mollusc and the two 'valves', or shells, are similar in shape, unlike those of the scallop which, however, they resemble in being radially ribbed.

There are ten other British species of cockle in the superfamily Cardiacea. The largest, growing to a length of 4 in., is the spiny cockle, or red-nose, Acanthocardia aculeata (Cardium aculeatum) found mainly on the South Devon coast. It is named for the spines along the ribs on its shell and for its cardinal-red foot. Another spined species, smaller and more widely distributed, is the prickly cockle A. echinata. There are other bivalves that are known as cockles, but belong to other groups of molluscs, including the large heart cockle, Glossus humanus, Cyprina islandica, Isocardia cor and others.

The 200 or so species of cockles in the Cardiacea have a world-wide distribution and 11 occur around the coasts of Britain. The edible cockle is found from high-

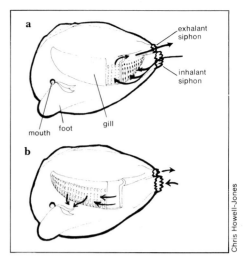

Above right: Cockle's siphon mechanism. **a:** Water is sucked in by one siphon and expelled by another, after passing through the gill. **b:** Trapped food drawn in with water is passed to the mouth by cilia. Below: Spiny cockle with siphon on right and pink foot showing between edges of mantle.

tide level down to 8 000 ft deep, lying obliquely not more than 2 in. below the surface of clean sand especially but also in mud or muddy gravel. Generally the average size increases from high to low water. It is particularly common in the sheltered waters of bays and the mouths of estuaries, as many as 10 000 having been recorded to a square metre. Although cockles do live in estuaries, the largest, about 2 in. long, are found far from fresh water. Dilution of the salt water with fresh has the curious effect of producing a less regularly shaped shell which is thinner and has fewer ribs than usual.

Digging with its foot

A cockle, in a most remarkable piece of behaviour for a mollusc, may sometimes skip upwards, bending in the middle its orange, tongue-like foot protruded between the two valves and pressing the tip into the sand before suddenly straightening it. Usually, however, this merely rolls the cockle over a few times. More often if the cockle has been dislodged and has to move it will creep along with its foot and re-bury itself.

It has been suggested that the 20–24 ribs that radiate out from the hinge region help to hold the cockle firmly in the mud or sand in which it is usually just buried, and that the globular shape helps to protect the animal should it be dislodged and rolled about by wave action.

At the back of the body is a pair of short tubes, or siphons, joined at the base like the legs of a pair of trousers. Water containing oxygen and the plankton and organic matter which are the food of the cockle, is drawn in through the lower one, that farthest from the hinge. Through the upper sweeps an outgoing jet, carrying wastes. The siphons are the only parts of the buried animal to project above the sand, and so they are an appropriate site for the eyes. These are small but surprisingly complex, with retinas and lenses, and are mounted on sensory tentacles. They enable the tentacles to be withdrawn if a shadow falls on them, so protecting them from predators, but presumably eyes can have little other use in such a sedentary, filter feeding animal.

To see what drives water through the siphons, one must open the valves which can be done when the cockle is clamped shut, by cutting through the two muscles, the adductors—one on each end and on either side of the hinge—that pull the valves together. If the cockle is dead, the valves may have already been forced partly open by the elastic ligament associated with the hinge which opposes the action of the muscles. The shell opened, the gills are revealed as a pair of flaps of tissue on each side of the foot, covered with countless tiny cilia whose beating sets up currents of water and propels the particles of food towards the mouth.

Usually a cockle stays in one place, and a tuft of algae may grow on it as if it were a stone. When the tide goes out the siphons are withdrawn but the site where the cockle is buried just below the sand may be revealed by the tuft of algae.

Close-up of a cockle's siphons shows the eye-bearing tentacles at their tips.

Conveyor belt digestion

Cockles feed on the small plant particles that abound in the water: single-celled plants such as diatoms and the spores and fragments of larger algae. There is little selection of what is eaten, however, and the stomach usually contains much sand and mud as well. The water bearing these particles enters through the lower end of one of the siphons and out by the other after passing through the fine latticework of the sieve-like gills. The cilia, as well as creating this current, also act to propel the trapped food towards the mouth, itself flanked by a pair of cilia-covered lips. In the stomach is a curious structure found in molluscs only, a rotating coiled rod 20–26 mm long called a 'crystalline style', turned by cilia lining the pocket which secretes it. The crystalline style, made up of digestive enzymes, gradually wears away and dissolves at the tip. Its rotation serves to draw along the food particles trapped in strings of mucus, as on a windlass, and at the same time its enzymes help to digest the food.

Chancy breeding

Though some related species are hermaphrodite, the sexes are separate in the edible cockle. Spawning begins at the end of February or early in March and continues till June or July, the eggs and milt being released freely into the water. Such eggs as become fertilised by this uncertain means develop into minute, free-swimming 'veliger' larvae, propelled by the beating of cilia. Eventually each develops a shell and foot, if it has not been eaten, and the resulting young cockles, still less than 1 mm long, settle on the sea bottom, some falling on stony ground and others on the sand or mud in which they can grow to maturity. The success of spawning varies from year to year and populations tend to be kept up by particularly good 'spat falls' perhaps once in 3 or 4 years.

As the shells grow, fine concentric grooves appear, marking former positions of the shell edge and providing a guide to age. The groove reflects the slower growth of the shell in winter when lack of sunshine means there is less plankton food available. A full-grown cockle has some 3–6 grooves and is about that many years old.

Cockle graveyard. Cockleshells are distinguished by their 20–24 radiating ribs.

Persecuted shellfish

For those cockles that escape man, life is still precarious, for they may be attacked by various parasites from within and by other creatures from without: snails that bore holes through their shells, starfish that pull open the valves by sheer persistence and push out their stomachs between them (see abalone, p. 11), gulls that attack when the tide is out and flatfish, like plaice and dab, when the tide is in. In addition, cockles can be stranded above high tide level by storms or carried away to other unsuitable areas. They may be killed, like other shore creatures, by excessive heat or cold as in the winter of 1904–5 when the Lancashire coasts were covered with ice floes and hundreds of tons of dead cockles were washed up the beach.

Athletic cockles

It has often been said that cockles can leap across the sand. A naturalist in the early years of this century used to entertain his friends with a story about cockles hitting him in the back. As he was walking up the beach he felt something, perhaps a stone, hit him in the small of the back. He turned about, to find nobody in sight. Continuing up the beach he was again hit in the back. Again he turned and could see nobody. This time, however, he saw one of the cockles leap, and realized what was happening. He did not say what kind of cockles they were, however.

Admittedly, this naturalist was not a tall man, but his story may have made up for his own lack of inches. From what we now know, the spiny cockle does leap, but to nothing like that extent. It has a very long red foot, much longer than most other cockles. When the tube-feet of a starfish, the cockle's hereditary enemy, touch its shell the spiny cockle leaps—for a distance of 8 in.

phylum	**Mollusca**
class	**Bivalvia**
subclass	**Lamellibranchia**
order	**Heterodonta**
family	**Cardiidae**
genus & species	***Cerastoderma edule** others*

Cock-of-the-rock

Two extremely ornate but uncommon South American birds which belong to the cotinga family, noted for the variety of wattles and crests worn by its several members. The two species of cock-of-the-rock are immediately recognisable by their crests that extend as a double fan from the base of the bill to the crown of the head. They are jay-sized birds, about 1 ft long, with short tails. The orange cock-of-the-rock is orange over most of its body except for the black and white flight feathers on the wings and a narrow chestnut stripe running around the margin of the crest. The rarer Peruvian cock-of-the-rock is a light red with grey-black wings and tail. The females of both species are a drab brown.

Birds of the forest floor

Cocks-of-the-rock live in the dense, damp forests of South America, in and around the Amazon basin. The orange cock-of-the-rock is found in the Guianas, Venezuela, northern Brazil and the southeast corner of Colombia. The Peruvian species live farther to the west and south and is found either side of the Andes in Colombia, Ecuador, Peru and Bolivia.

The most likely place to find cocks-of-the-rock is in forest areas where there are rocky outcrops, which provide shallow caverns for nesting. The birds live near the floor of the forest rather than in the canopy, and have the strong legs and claws associated with a bird that spends its time on or near the ground.

Feeding

Cotingas are mainly fruit eaters, and cocks-of-the-rock are no exception, but they also eat insects, spending a large part of their time searching for them on the ground. Where cocks-of-the-rock have been kept in captivity it has been found that they quickly lose condition and die if insect food has not been provided. Besides insects, captive birds have been found to relish snails, which they open by smashing the shells against a rock.

Gaudy males compete for mates

The cocks-of-the-rock are among the many birds in which the male takes the minimum part in breeding. Like the capercaillie, the male cock-of-the rock has nothing to do with nesting, once he has mated. A feature of these birds is that the males have developed elaborate display rituals and ornate, often bizarre, plumage. This accentuates the displays with which they challenge other males and beckon the females.

A displaying cock-of-the-rock is so bizarre that at first sight it is hard to believe that it is a bird. The bill and tail become covered by the crest and other ornate plumage obscuring the form of the body. When the display starts, the crest is fanned out so that the two halves spread over the bill. At the same time, the feathers of the back and breast are fluffed out and the tail coverts—the feathers at the base of the tail—are fanned out. These feathers are very fluffy and stand out, so the

bird looks as if it is wrapped in a shawl, which shimmers in the slightest breeze.

The males have traditional displaying grounds, or arenas, where as many as 40 birds gather. Within the arena each bird has a 'private' perch on a branch near the ground and a 'lek' or patch of cleared ground 1 ft or so across. The ground in the lek is cleared of dead leaves by the violent draughts caused by the owner landing and taking off. The occupants of an arena regularly gather in the breeding season to display. As well as displaying their brilliant plumage, they have a variety of calls and movements. They bob their heads, showing off the crest, and hop about the perches, flicking their wings. Together with bugle-like calls uttered as the birds arrive at the arena, they make two mechanical noises. One is a finger-snapping sound made with the bill as the head bobs and the other is made when the birds are chasing each other on the wing. One of the wing feathers has a modified tip that vibrates to produce a whistling sound when the bird is flying.

When a female visits the arena the males immediately drop to their leks and display. The female watches the displays for a few minutes then flies down to the male of her choice, hitting the ground by him and immediately taking off again. He follows after her and they mate away from the lek.

The females build their nests in caves and under overhangs on cliffs. Several nests may be built within a few feet of each other and the females roost on the nests even when not incubating or brooding. The nests are made of mud bound with vines and roots and may weigh up to $8\frac{1}{2}$ lb.

Two eggs are laid but, because of the rarity of the cocks-of-the-rock and the difficulty of penetrating their jungle habitat, little or nothing is known about the raising of the young.

Neighbours drift apart

The orange cock-of-the-rock is presumed to be the ancestor of the Peruvian species. This spread south into sub-tropical zones from the tropical forests where its forerunner lived. The home of the Peruvian cock-of-the-rock is now on the slopes and valleys of the Andes, and since it became separated from the orange species, the Peruvian species has diverged into two subspecies,

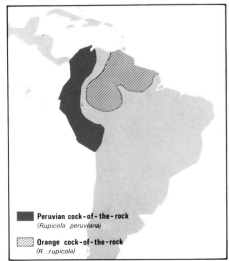

Peruvian cock-of-the-rock
(*Rupicola peruviana*)

Orange cock-of-the-rock
(*R. rupicola*)

Klaus Paysan

Left: Orange cocks-of-the-rock are natives of the Central and South American rain forests.
Above: The glaring orange cock-of-the-rock, whose bill is surmounted by a helmet-like crest.

or races, which live on each side of the mountains. *Rupicola peruviana sanguinolenta* lives on the west, while *Rupicola peruviana aurea* lives on the east. The differences between them are only slight, but they have been made possible by the complete isolation of the two populations by the temperate climate of the Andes range. If there had been passes through the mountains, low enough to allow a belt of tropical vegetation to run between east and west, the subspecies probably would not have arisen, because the populations would have mixed and interbred. Cocks-of-the-rock are not the only animals to have become separated in this way. The fishes in the rivers and streams on either side of the Andes have similar characteristics, the populations on each side having evolved independently from common ancestors. The differences between the east and west populations are only slight,

because the Andes were thrown up comparatively recently. Between 30 and 45 million years ago, movements in the earth's crust threw up the Alps, Himalayas and Rockies as well as the Andes. Where a geographical upheaval has isolated populations in this way, a study reveals information on the rate at which evolution proceeds. In the Andes, where conditions are similar on both sides, the cocks-of-the-rock have altered very little in 30-odd million years.

class	**Aves**
order	**Passeriformes**
family	**Cotingidae**
genus & species	***Rupicola rupicola*** *Orange cock-of-the-rock* ***R. peruviana*** *Peruvian cock-of-the-rock*

Cockroach

Cockroaches used to be classified together with the grasshoppers, crickets, stick-insects and others in one large order, the Orthoptera. This has now been split up into several separate orders of which one, the Dictyoptera, comprises the praying mantises and the cockroaches.

These are fairly large insects, flattened in shape, with two pairs of wings, the fore-wings being more or less thickened and leathery, serving as a protective cover for the delicate hindwings, just as the hardened forewings or elytra of beetles do. The hindwings of cockroaches are pleated like a fan when not in use; when expanded for flight they have a very large surface area. In the commonest British species, the black beetle as it is called, the male has very small wings, the female has mere vestiges, and neither can fly. The female has reduced wings and is flightless in some of the other species also.

The most familiar of the 3 500 species of cockroaches are those tropical and sub-tropical forms which have taken advantage of the warmth and the opportunities for scavenging afforded by homes and premises in which food is made or stored. By this means they have extended their range into temperate and cold regions, and some of them have been artificially distributed all over the world. In the wild state, the great majority of species are tropical. In the outdoor fauna of Britain they are represented by 3 small species only, belonging to one genus, Ectobius.

There are 6 introduced indoor species of cockroach known in Britain of which the following three are the most common:
Common cockroach, or **black beetle** Blatta orientalis *length variable, averaging about 1 in., dark brown (females almost black) wings not reaching the tip of the body in the male, vestigial in the female; both sexes flightless. A common pest in house. Now cosmopolitan in distribution, the region of its origin is unknown.*
German cockroach, steamfly or **shiner** Blatella germanica *about ½ in. long, yellowish-brown with two dark brown stripes on the prothorax, or fore-part, of the body. Wings fully developed. Almost as abundant as the common cockroach and certainly not of German origin; probably a native of North Africa.*
American cockroach Periplaneta americana *males nearly 1½ in. long, reddish-brown, with fully developed wings. Found mostly in sea port towns and on ships. In tropical countries it is the chief house-living cockroach. It is not an American insect and probably also originated in North Africa.*

They come out at night
In the wild, most cockroaches live on the ground among decaying vegetation or be-

Kitchen nightmare: a common cockroach has a wash and brush-up after a meal of bread. These household pests have the depressing habit of fouling far more than they actually eat.

Newly-moulted cockroach larva. It may moult 6 – 12 times before it is fully grown.

hind dead bark, and are coloured brown to match their surroundings. The 'domestic' species probably all lived in this way once. Some cockroaches are found among growing plants and are patterned in brown, yellow or green. The ground-living cockroaches are nocturnal, hiding away by day and coming out at night, just as the house-living ones do. Some of the large tropical species fly freely at night and are attracted to artificial light.

Their flattened bodies allow them to creep into cracks and crevices; in houses, cockroaches hide in inaccessible places and are not easy to get rid of.

Poisoned baits may be effective if used persistently, and insecticidal powders and sprays kill them if introduced well into their hiding places. Bad infestations are best dealt with by professional pest controllers.

Unwelcome scavengers

In the wild, most cockroaches are scavengers on dead insect and other animal remains, fallen fruit and fungi; the transition to scavenging in human habitations is easy and obvious. Some of the wild species feed on wood, which they are able to digest with the help of protozoans, microscopical one-celled animals, in their intestine. Termites, which are closely allied to cockroaches, eat and digest wood by the same means.

In houses, cockroaches will eat any kind of human food that they can get at. They will also eat a variety of substances not generally regarded as edible, such as book-bindings, boot-blacking, ink and whitewash. Frank Buckland, in his *Curiosities of Natural History*, tells of a gentleman on his way home from India by ship who was much annoyed by cockroaches. At night, when he was asleep they 'came and devoured the little rims of white skin at the roots of the finger nails'. The harm they do is greatly increased by their habit of fouling, with their droppings, far more than they actually eat. The only good that can be said of them is that so far as is known they do not convey any disease.

Breeding

The eggs are enclosed in a purse-like capsule called the ootheca. In the common cockroach this is carried for a day or two, protruding from the body of the female, and then dropped, or sometimes stuck in a crevice, after which the insect takes no further notice of it. It is white when it first appears at the tip of her abdomen, but darkens later and, when deposited, is almost black and rather less than ½ in. long. Normally an ootheca contains 16 eggs in 2 neat rows of 8, but there may be more or less than this. The eggs hatch 2−3 months after the formation of the ootheca, which splits to allow the young to emerge. The young of the common cockroach are about ⅕ in. long on hatching, and white, gradually becoming brown as they grow. They resemble their parents in form, except that the wings are lacking, and take 10 months −1 year to reach maturity. Moulting of the skin, or ecdysis, takes place anything from 6−12 times in the course of growth. The breeding habits of the American cockroach are similar.

In the German cockroach the ootheca is carried by the female until a day or less before hatching, and the eggs may even hatch

A brace of American cockroaches. Unlike the common cockroach, the American version has fully-developed wings. Despite its name it is not an American insect: it probably originated in North Africa.

Jane Burton: Photo Res.

Anthony Bannister: NHPA

JAL Cooke

while it is still attached to her. It is chestnut brown and, a few days before hatching, a green band appears along each side of it. Hatching usually takes place 4—6 weeks after the ootheca is formed and it normally contains 35—45 eggs.

Cockroaches: living fossils in the home

In a manner of speaking the world went wild with delight when the coelacanth, a living fossil, first came to light. The same intense interest would be shown if another living fossil were to be discovered. There is something in the psychology of these events which recalls the parable of the pieces of silver that were thought lost and were found again. Nobody but the most devoted scientist, however, would think of rolling out the red carpet for the roaches. Yet they are extremely interesting and primitive insects.

Many fossils have been found showing that there were already many species and abundant populations of roaches at the time when coal measures were being deposited, 300 million years ago. These cock-

roaches of the Carboniferous period differed little from the present day ones and the family as a whole must be regarded as insects which, by adopting a simple and secure way of life at an early period of the earth's history, and never departing from it, have inherited the earth by their very meekness. As an example of success in survival they have few equals, but because they intrude themselves on our notice in such an unpleasant manner, few people find themselves able to regard them highly. Nevertheless, there are a few people whose sole purpose in life is to rear cockroaches.

Partly because they are so easy to obtain and partly because their structure and anatomy is so simple and generalised, cockroaches are widely used to introduce students to the science of entomology, and breeding them for this purpose is one of the less well-known human occupations.

phylum	**Arthropoda**
class	**Insecta**
order	**Dictyoptera**
family	**Blattidae**

Hated and loathed as a household pest because of its habit of defiling food, the cockroach is nevertheless one of the best examples of success in surviving; and it has an important role in the teaching of entomology.
This close-up shows the organs of special sense: the eyes, which are compound, consisting of many small elements; the palps and antennae, which are organs of touch. On the highly mobile antennae are structures which are used for smelling. Above the front of the 'shell' are the semi-transparent elytra, or wing cases.

The cod is a voracious eater taking other fish and invertebrates. Even keys, a partridge and a book have been found in a cod's stomach.

Cod

The cod is the second most valuable food fish in the world, after the herring. The cod family contains 150 species, of which a dozen are valuable food fishes, including the coalfish, haddock, hake, ling, pollack and whiting, each of which we shall deal with in turn.

The Atlantic cod is round-bodied, up to 211 lb weight and 6 ft long, although those usually sold are 2½–25 lb. Its colour is olive-green to brown, the back and flanks marbled with spots, the belly silvery. There are 3 dorsal and 2 anal fins. The snout projects over the mouth and there is a whisker-like barbel on the throat.

Local populations
The distribution of cod is shown by the main fisheries: North Sea, Norway, Bear Island, Iceland, Greenland, Newfoundland and Labrador. The closely related Alaska cod lives in the north Pacific where, it has been predicted, there may some day be a large commercial fishery. Cod live on the continental shelf, at depths of 60–600 ft, although the bulk of the catch is taken in depths of 60 to 240 ft, on long lines, each carrying snoods bearing hooks. A single line may be 12 000 ft long. At times they can be caught as close as 50 yd off shore.

Within each area, such as the North Sea, Norway, Iceland and so on, the populations of cod are self-contained, but there are long migrations of several hundred miles by the larger fishes between the areas, for example

from Newfoundland to Greenland, Greenland to Iceland. Within each area there are feeding grounds and spawning grounds between which the cod move with the seasons. In autumn they come into the shallower inshore waters, but move temporarily into deeper water when feeding, and are then mainly bottom-feeders. In summer they feed farther out still, mainly on smaller fishes.

There is also a daily movement which is related to the intensity of light, similar to that found in a number of other shoaling fishes. Even at depths of 600 ft, the cod form compact shoals during the daylight hours, disperse at sunset and re-form at sunrise.

Eats like an ostrich
The main food of cod is other fishes, especially herring, mackerel and haddock, as well as sand eels. Squid are eaten in fair quantity and also bottom-living invertebrates such as shrimps, crabs, molluscs and worms. It is not surprising, therefore, to find that cod have strong sharply-pointed teeth, nor that their digestive juices dissolve seashells and the shells of crabs. But their voracity seems to know no bounds. Articles taken from stomachs of cod include a bunch of keys, a hare, a partridge, a black guillemot, a white turnip, a book bound in calf and a long piece of tallow candle!

Millions of eggs
There is no marked outward difference between the sexes, which become sexually mature at 4–5 years when 2–3 ft long. In the first 3 months of the year they move to the spawning grounds. This may take them across very deep water, for example

from Norway to Bear Island, or Iceland to Greenland.

The females shed their eggs and the males their milt into the sea, where fertilisation is random. A well-grown female lays 4–6 million eggs, $\frac{1}{20}$ in. diameter, which float to the surface. In 10–20 days these hatch and the larvae, $\frac{1}{4}$ in. long, remain in the surface plankton for the next 2½ months. At just over $\frac{3}{4}$ in. long they move down to the bottom, in depths of about 240 ft, to feed on small crustaceans, amphipods, isopods and small crabs. As they grow they move into deeper water. At the end of the year the young cod is 6 in. long, and 1 ft long a year later. Young cod of these sizes keep together in age groups, and are known as codling.

Only one need survive
Fishes that lay large numbers of eggs are beset by enemies and other natural hazards. Only one of the 4–6 million eggs laid by the female cod need survive to keep the population steady. Many eggs fail to be fertilised, and these and many of the fertilised eggs are eaten by other fishes as well as smaller predators in the plankton. All are at the mercy of winds and currents, large numbers being cast ashore or killed off by changes of temperature. Damage to the fry is similar, and when the young fishes go down to the bottom, other predatory fishes continue the slaughter.

Cod fry are among several species of fishes that take refuge under the umbrella and among the stinging tentacles of large blue jellyfishes. Even so, some brush against the tentacles and are paralysed and eaten by the jellyfish. Even those not lost by these accidents enjoy no more than a temporary immunity from attack by larger fishes.

Mansell

Engraving of fishermen fishing for cod from a dory or flat-bottomed boat off Newfoundland.

J Allan Cash

△ *The fleet waiting. Codfishing boats at Henningsvaer, Lofoten Islands, Norway.*
▽ *Cod drying in the sun. The skin yields glue, the swimbladder isinglass and its liver high grade oil.*

J Allan Cash

Fish makes history

Cod have been fished in quantity since the 16th century and in this century the annual catch has reached 3–400 million fish. As a source of revenue they have had an important bearing on the course of human history. At the beginning of the 16th century, Spanish, Basque, French and English fishermen were catching cod in the North Sea and North Atlantic. Many sailors fighting the Spanish Armada had learned seamanship in the cod ships. Already in 1536, however, Jacques Cartier had pushed across the North Atlantic, a 6-month journey in those days, to discover the islands of St Pierre and Miquelon, on the Grand Banks of Newfoundland. A century later there were 300 French ships fishing for cod off these islands, together with Spanish and Dutch fishermen.

England was slow to exploit these silver mines, as the seemingly inexhaustible supplies of cod off Newfoundland were called. Early in the 17th century, however, there came a two-pronged attack. Ships from Bristol and the Devon ports were making the long journey and returning with valuable cargoes of salted cod. By 1634 an estimated 18 680 English seamen were working the Newfoundland fishery. The colonists of New England had also discovered this source of wealth and by 1635, one generation after the colony was founded, 24 vessels were bringing back up to 300 000 cod a year, and the first export from Massachusetts was a cargo of cod.

Cod led the English and the French to Canada, to a long trail of strife, and when the United States was founded a title to the cod-fishing ground was included in the Act of Independence. The cod appears on bank notes, seals, coins and revenue stamps of the New England colonies, and a carved figure of a cod still occupies a place of honour in the Massachusetts State House. The fish left its mark on the history of the fishing grounds, in the form of open strife between crews of different nations.

Salted cod early became a standby for seamen, explorers and armies during the period when Europeans were spreading out into the new found continents. Nothing of the fish was wasted. Its skin yielded glue, its swimbladder furnished isinglass, its liver gave a high-grade oil. Even cods' tongues, originally cut out and strung on wires as a tally of the daily catch, were salted in barrels.

By 1770, cod liver oil was being used for poultices and as a medicament for the sick and aged. By 1820 it was being used against rickets, a disease linked with town life in the Industrial Revolution. It was considered useless by many medical men, and it was not until 1921 that the value of cod liver oil in the treatment of rickets was set beyond doubt.

class	**Osteichthyes**
order	**Gadiformes**
family	**Gadidae**
genus & species	***Gadus morhua***

Coelacanth

First made known to science in 1938, and belonging to an order previously thought to have become extinct 70 million years ago, the coelacanth is a 5ft long, 120lb primitive fish. Coelacanth means hollow spines, referring to those of the fins. The fish, first caught off the coast of Natal, and later off Madagascar, is of robust build, brown to dark blue, and outwardly shows several peculiarities. The first is that each of the pectoral fins, instead of coming straight off the body, is carried on scaly muscular lobes and seems to be halfway between a normal fin and the walking limb of primitive land animals. The rear dorsal and the anal fins are similarly lobed. The second peculiarity is in the tail. Instead of the junction between the body and the tail fin being marked by a constriction, the body merely narrows rapidly and evenly, and then continues backwards as a narrow strip, dividing the rays of the tail fin into two equal parts, one above and one below it. Another peculiarity is its scales. Each scale is a bony plate covered with dermal denticles (small tooth-like points in the skin) like those of sharks.

Scientists' clever forecast

In addition to its strange external appearance the coelacanth has a number of peculiar internal features which are just as significant as its ancient ancestry. Although it is a bony fish, the backbone is made up almost entirely of a large, tough cartilaginous rod, the notochord. In an evolutionary sense, the notochord came before the backbone, and in the developing embryo of vertebrates it appears first and is later enclosed by the vertebrae and lost, except in very primitive vertebrates (for example, lampreys). The heart of the coelacanth is very simple, even simpler than that of other fishes. Interestingly enough it is like the heart predicted by anatomists when trying to explain how the heart evolved.

The kidneys, instead of lying just under the backbone, are on the floor of the abdomen, and instead of being a pair they are joined. This is unique, and it is hard to see any explanation. It is not so much a primitive character as one quite unexpected. The stomach also is peculiar; it is just a large bag. The intestine has a spiral valve, a feature shared with sharks and other primitive fishes.

Armoured 'lungs'

Perhaps one of the more perplexing features of the coelacanth is the swimbladder. As we have seen in dealing with the coalfish (p. 590), this probably arose in the first place as a breathing organ. The fossil coelacanths, which flourished 450–70 million years ago, had a swimbladder and lobed fins. It was largely among these fishes that scientists looked for a possible ancestor to the land vertebrates. That is, the coelacanths seemed to be distant ancestors of man, with the beginnings of lungs and of walking limbs. One drawback to such a theory was that the

Highlight in natural history: Professor Smith poses with Malania, *the second coelacanth to be discovered, together with South African Air Force personnel, Captain Hunt's schooner crew, and the French governor of the Comores (at right). The date is December 29, 1952.*

swimbladder of coelacanths was sheathed in bony scales, so it could not have served as a lung and it would have made a very poor hydrostatic organ.

Hopes frustrated

When it was realised that an actual living coelacanth had been found, the more sober scientists hoped it would shed light on the puzzle of the rigid swimbladder. The more excitable ones began to talk about the living coelacanth shedding light on man's ancestry. Some of them broadcast to this effect and the coelacanth became, in the minds of many listeners, a missing link of supreme importance. That proved, however, a nine days' wonder. The swimbladder was also a disappointment. The first modern coelacanth was almost decomposed before being examined by an expert. In addition it had been gutted in the hope of preserving it. When more living coelacanths were caught and dissected, the swimbladder was found to be slender and filled with fat. It, also, cannot function as a lung and even more certainly is not a hydrostatic organ.

There are a number of other features of the anatomy which are peculiar, and which are of interest mainly to the expert. To-

gether they suggest that the coelacanths were an aberrant offshoot of the early fishes, having gone off at a tangent from the main line of evolution. They show relationships with sharks, chimaera, lungfishes, and other primitive fishes. Above all, they indicate that the coelacanths, following an independent evolutionary line, were a dying race, with the living coelacanth as the last survivor, so far as we know.

One of the peculiarities, which has an interesting lesson to teach, is the skull. This is hinged midway, as in fossil coelacanths. The brain cavity in it is large. It has long been a puzzle how the brain managed to work if the skull containing it was hinged. The living coelacanth shows that the brain is small and confined to the rear portion of the skull, behind the hinge. It lies embedded in fat and cushioned on two large blood ducts. The brain itself is therefore very small by comparison with the cavity of the skull.

It is common, in studying fossil animals, to take a plaster cast of the cranial cavity in the skull to reconstruct the shape and proportions of the brain. The living coelacanth teaches us that this could well be misleading.

Trawler's lucky catch

A considerate and curious seaman, a quick-thinking curator of a tiny museum, and a scientist who let nothing stand in his way: these three people brought to light one of the most exciting animals of the century. On December 22, 1938, a fishing boat shot her trawl off the mouth of the Chalumna River, west of East London, in South Africa. It was not the usual place for the trawlers to fish. On this occasion the ship stood 3 miles offshore, her trawl dragging the seabed at 120 ft. It came up with 3 tons of fish, which were emptied on the deck in the usual way. Half an hour later the trawlermen came to the last fish, 5 ft long, blue, and with unusual scales, a fish they had not seen before. It lived for 4 hours.

The skipper, Captain Goosen, realising he had something unusual, sent the fish to Miss Courtenay-Latimer, curator at the East London museum. She wrote to Professor JLB Smith at Grahamstown, 400 miles away. But it was now Christmas Eve, the mail was choked, and so Smith did not see the fish for some days after its capture. Nevertheless, although it was in poor shape he realised its importance, and it is to the credit of Smith, Miss Courtenay-Latimer and Captain Goosen that a priceless scientific treasure was brought to the notice of the world's scientists.

On December 20, 1952, a fisherman, Ahmed Hussein, landed a 5ft, 100lb fish with a hook and line, from 65 ft of water off the Comores Islands, west of Madagascar. Professor Smith was informed, and flew to the Comores in a South African Air Force Dakota placed at his disposal by the then Prime Minister, Dr Malan. Although Smith gave it the name *Malania anjouanae* after the Prime Minister, it was later realised this was the same as the first coelacanth, which had been named *Latimeria chalumnae*, after Miss Courtenay-Latimer. This second fish was the culmination of a 14-year campaign in which Smith flooded East Africa with leaflets in English, French and Portuguese, offering a reward of 10 000 Escudos for the next two specimens caught.

A lucky find

Madagascar, including the Comores, was then under French administration, and French scientists now took up the search. A third was found in September, 1953, and in 1954 two more were caught: on January 28 and January 31. Since then others have been caught, which suggests that the one caught off Natal in 1938 had wandered from its normal habitat—a lucky accident for students of fishes. Skin-divers have looked for the fish off the coasts of Madagascar and neighbouring islands, and some have caught a glimpse of large fishes believed to be coelacanths, along the steep slopes where the rocky sea-bed suddenly dips in a vertical wall to very deep water.

This, one of the most interesting of living fishes, is known therefore almost entirely from a dozen dead individuals examined by scientists, or watched for the very short while a few survived in aquaria. Brought to the surface they have soon died due to the combination of decompression and exposure to warmer waters.

△ *The leaflet which offered East African fishermen 10 000 Escudos for the next two coelacanths.*

▽ *The coelacanth sketches and notes made by Miss M Courtenay-Latimer (left).*

Cavalier treatment

Right at the beginning of this article on the coelacanth we used the phrase 'first made known to science in 1938'. People often say the coelacanth was unknown until 1938. It was only unknown to western civilization. It seems a reasonable guess that the fishermen of the Madagascar region have known it for hundreds, possibly thousands, of years. They call it *Kombessa*. They regard it as a poor food fish unless salted and dried.

Its skin is slimy, and when caught it continues oozing oil. They have used its scales as 'sandpaper', when mending bicycle tyres!

class	**Osteichthyes**
order	**Actinistia**
family	**Coelacanthidae**
genus & species	*Latimeria chalumnae*

'Old Fourlegs'

Coelacanths are deep-water fishes, strong, heavy in the body, and weighing up to about 160 lb. 'Old Fourlegs', as it was dubbed by Professor Smith, has mobile pectoral and pelvic fins which resemble stalked flippers. These probably help the coelacanth to creep along the seabed, hunting by stealth and cunning. And the characteristic double tail, found in no modern fish, is a link with the Rhipidistian fishes of 320 million years ago, the supposed ancestors of land animals.
▷ Skeleton of a coelacanth tail. 'Coelacanth' means 'hollow spine', and the fish indeed has fins made up of rays of hollow cartilage.
▽ X-ray of the second dorsal fin of a coelacanth, showing the hollow rays of the fin and upper tail. In Malania—named after the South African Prime Minister who provided a military aircraft for Professor Smith's dash to the Comores in 1952—there was only one dorsal; this is now regarded as an aberrant type.

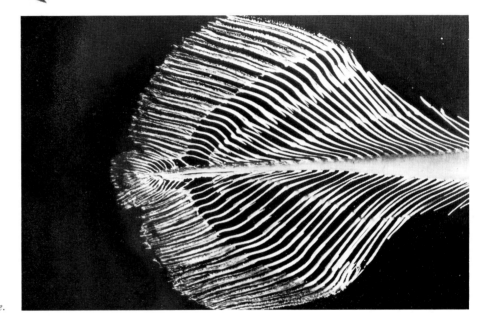

All photos supplied by Centre de Documentation du CNRS

Collared dove perching on rooftop. Although it usually nests in trees, it will sometimes select a roof or window sill for nesting.

Brian Hawkes NHPA

Collared dove

This is one of the smaller doves, measuring about 11 in. from bill tip to tail tip. This is slightly larger than the turtle dove, from which it is distinguished by a narrow black collar around the back of its neck and more conspicuous white on the underside of the tail. The upper parts are pale brown and the head and underparts pale grey. It has pale blue-grey shoulders which show in flight. The blackish primary wing feathers are also a distinguishing feature.

The collared dove, or collared turtle dove, can easily be confused with the semi-domesticated barbary dove or bronze ring-dove. The latter is derived from the African pink-headed dove which, however, is considered by some ornithologists to belong to the same species as the collared dove.

A gift of the gods

Originally the collared dove was a bird of Asia and Africa ranging from Korea and northern China, across India to the Middle East, around the southern end of the Red Sea and across the southern borders of the Sahara Desert. It colonised the island of Honshu, Japan, early in the 19th century, where it escaped from captivity, and in recent times has rapidly spread across Europe. It is a bird of farmlands, gardens and villages, and in many parts it is common in the centres of cities.

The call is a three-syllable *coo-coo-cook* with the accent on the second syllable. There is a Greek legend that the call advertised the meanness of a lady who employed a maid for a miserly 18 pieces a year. The girl prayed to the gods asking them to let the world know of her drudgery. Zeus took pity on her and created the collared dove that calls *deca-octo* or *ten-eight*. Although not much like the dove's call this story has given the collared dove its name, *Streptopelia decaocto*.

Gleaning doves

In their spread across Europe, collared doves are very much dependent on man for a large part of their food, as their diet is mainly spilt seeds lying on the ground, added to the naturally occurring grass seeds. Man scatters cereal seeds about in his farmyards and poultry runs and there is plenty left lying in stubble fields. In winter the collared doves gather in flocks of a hundred or more to feed on this bounty.

The tips of grass shoots and seed heads are also eaten. Some fruit is taken: snowberries that have been knocked down by other birds are sometimes eaten in winter, and it seems that collard doves are becoming pests of cherry orchards in Europe.

Rapid breeding

Nests are usually made in trees, of many species, preferably conifers. They are placed near the trunk from 6–60 ft above the ground. Occasionally nests are found on roofs and window sills, and in a few in-

614

stances the abandoned nests of turtle doves and woodpigeons are used as foundations. The male helps the female with the nest building, collecting twigs from the ground or snapping them off the branches with the beak and taking them to the female, who does the actual construction. After the twigs have been laid, the nest is finished off with a lining of grass and roots.

During courtship there is a spectacular display flight in which the doves soar up, clapping their wings together over their backs, then glide down, often in a spiral, with wings and tail spread, showing the conspicuous black and white of the tail feathers.

Two white eggs are laid, rarely three, and occasionally one in late clutches. They are incubated for 14—16 days. Both sexes share in the incubation, and, as is usual in doves and pigeons, the male sits during the day and the female by night. In India the male's day shift was found to be from 10 am to 4 pm while the female had an 18-hour night shift.

The chicks spend 2—3 weeks on the nest and are fed for the first few days on pigeon's milk secreted from the adults' crop. Pigeon's milk is a cheesy fluid, very rich in proteins and fat, and to obtain it the chicks push their heads down the parents' throat. When they are a few days old, the milk is supplemented with grain and other seeds. A suggested function of pigeon's milk is to supply protein almost lacking in a diet of seeds. Pigeons do not provide their chicks with insects, which other seed-eating birds collect to give their offspring the protein necessary for rapid growth.

In northern Europe collared doves breed from March to September, and in mild weather this may be extended each way to January and November.

As the young birds leave the nest they form flocks which increase as doves from later broods join them. On average, only one chick will survive from each brood, but it still allows for a rapid increase.

Explosive increase across Europe

Collared doves became established in south-east Europe in the 18th century, but whether they spread there naturally, or were introduced by the Turks, is not known. There they stayed for 2 centuries, then in the early part of the 20th century they exploded westward, so that by 1967 they had reached the very western parts of Europe and were breeding in Fair Isle, in the Scilly Isles and in Ireland.

The movement was a steady one to north-west. In 1912 there were collared doves in Belgrade, in 1930 they had reached Hungary, and in 1943 Vienna. By 1948 they had been seen in Denmark, crossing the Skagerrak into Sweden in 1949. In Britain the first collared doves to arrive bred in Norfolk in 1955. Since then the population, aided by immigrants, has rapidly expanded. By 1964 it was estimated at 19 000 and collared doves were to be found in most of England and many parts of Scotland, Wales and Ireland. Their numbers are still increasing and there are fears that they may become as much of

Pair of collared doves. Both partners build the nest, incubate the eggs and feed the young. They have recently spread across Europe, and these were photographed in a London suburb.

Hugh Maynard

a pest as the woodpigeon through their attacks on young grasses, seeds and fruits.

Collared doves are not the only birds to have extended their range across Europe in recent times. Serins have spread considerably, grey wagtails spread into northern Germany and Scandinavia during the last century, and Syrian woodpeckers have moved up the Danube. The basis for the spread is probably the general improvement of the European climate. The winters are less severe, so that non-migratory birds like the collared dove can survive in their new homes during the winter. Their survival, however, was only possible because of the ample food supplies around farms and villages. The collared dove could not live in northern Europe without man, and the rate at which it spread may have been accelerated by the expansion of European agriculture.

Whatever the reason, however, the story of the collared dove serves to show that zoology is a dynamic subject; animals and their habits are continually changing under the influence of a varying environment. It is essential that the changes both in the environment and the animal be understood before we take any action to influence either. To ignore them, as has been done in the past, is to encourage dangerous shifts in the delicate balances between animals and environments.

class	**Aves**
order	**Columbiformes**
family	**Columbidae**
genus & species	***Streptopelia decaocto***

615

Colobus monkey

Little is known of the three species of colobus monkey or guereza, because they are shy, live in dense foliage, and nowhere in their range are they common. The best known is the black colobus that has short, black fur with long plumes of white on the tail and running down the sides. There is also white on the chin, cheeks and forehead. The black colobus was once divided into many species but now it is thought that there are many variations in the coat of the one species. As so little is known about them, however, it could be that there is more than one species. In one form the monkeys have long whiskers, a whorl of hair on the head and only a small tuft on the tail. Another is similar but has no white fur while a third has white fur but no whorl. The red colobus is another species, with a black body and chestnut head, arms and legs. The olive colobus was once placed in a separate genus.

Colobus monkeys measure about $3\frac{1}{2}-5$ ft, of which over half is tail. The thumbs are absent or very small, which accounts for the name of colobus, derived from the Greek for mutilated.

Shy tree-dwellers

Colobus monkeys live in Africa from Senegal across to Ethiopia and down to Angola. They live in dense forests, rarely coming down from the trees. The olive colobus sometimes feeds on the ground, otherwise they usually come down only to visit saltlicks. They live in family groups of up to about 20, led by an old male. Each group has a territory, the boundaries of which are defended by threatening calls and, in the case of the black colobus, showing off the striking pattern of the coat, although the black and white coat is said to act as camouflage at other times. The monkeys' reaction to fear is to hide, and they are apparently very difficult to see as the plumes and black and white patterns blend in well with sun-dappled vegetation.

Usually the group stays near the centre of its territory. The members of one group that was studied had a 30-acre territory but kept mainly to a central 9-acre part where they followed regular tracks. They set off in search of food at sunrise, returning to the sleeping trees just before sunset.

Specialised leaf-eaters

Colobus monkeys eat the foliage of forest trees. Some kinds are preferred, and young, tender leaves are specially selected. Digestion of coarse leaves, which are not very nutritious, is improved by the complex stomach, which is divided into pouches, rather like the stomachs of cattle.

Promiscuous monkeys

Apart from one monkey being leader there is no social order in a colobus group. This means that any male is free to mate with

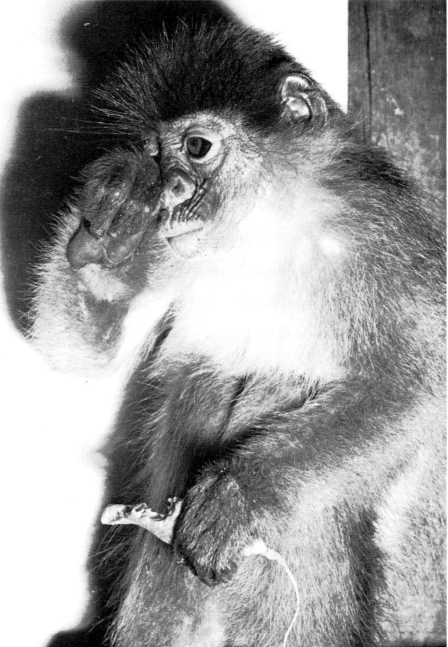

any female. When a female is on heat she may mate with several males in quick succession. Just before giving birth she leaves the group. The newborn baby, which is white all over, is held in her arms at first, but when it is 2 weeks old it can cling to her back as she climbs through the trees with the rest of the group. At 6 weeks the baby begins to eat leaves, but it is not fully weaned until 7 months old, when it leaves its mother and joins the other youngsters.

The olive colobus is most unusual among monkeys in that the female carries her newborn baby in her mouth. Only several weeks later does it cling to her fur. This habit may be due to the shortness of her fur, which prevents a very young baby getting a grip.

Eaten by chimpanzees

Man and eagles are the colobus' main enemies but they have been seen to be eaten by chimpanzees. Jane Goodall, who studied chimpanzees in the wild, once saw a young

Colobus monkeys have short forelimbs and long-haired coats. Living in dense foliage, they are very hard to see—especially as their fur has good camouflage properties. They are slower-moving than other monkeys

chimpanzee shoot up a tree and pounce on one of a group of colobus sitting there. Other chimpanzees followed it and they shared the carcase between them.

When threatened a group may abuse the intruder, shaking branches and nodding their heads. Otherwise they will try to hide or flee down one of their tracks, in no particular order except that the leader brings up the rear.

In touch with the heavens

Colobus fur with its long plumes is used by certain African tribes for ceremonial capes, headdresses and shields, and in the past Arab traders carried furs to Central

V Reynolds

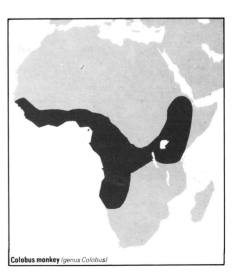
Douglas Fisher

Asia where the naturally glossy black fur with white plumes was greatly valued. From Asia samples found their way to the furriers of Venice who tore them apart to find out how Oriental craftsmen managed to fix white plumes into the short black fur. Then, in the 19th century, the fur became popular in Europe. With the advent of firearms the Africans were able to supply an expanding market, and by 1892 175 000 skins were exported to Europe alone. These were perfect, commercially valuable skins, so, allowing for the number damaged, the slaughter of monkeys must have been terrific. According to Arab legend, some skins were ruined by the monkeys themselves. It was said that if a monkey was wounded it would tear its skin to pieces rather than let the hunter profit. This would mean incredible foresight on the part of the monkey, but as legend also had it that they were messengers of the gods this is not so surprising. The colobus monkeys were credited with this high office because of their habit of ascending to the tops of high trees at sunrise and sunset, and sitting silently as if in prayer.

class	**Mammalia**
order	**Primates**
family	**Cercopithecidae**
genus & species	**Colobus polykomos** black colobus **C. badius** red colobus **C. verus** olive colobus

△ Left: *A black colobus meditates among the treetops. With the Arabs, the colobus got the reputation of being a messenger of the gods because of its habit of climbing trees and sitting as if in reverence at morning and evening prayer-time.*
△ *Male red colobus from west Africa.*
▽ *Baby colobus, only a few days old, steels itself to tackle a blade of grass. The colobus helps its vegetable diet on its way by means of its cow-like pouched stomach.*

J Verschuren WWF

Colobus monkey *(genus Colobus)*

Colorado beetle

Familiar to many people from the pictures displayed in police stations and elsewhere, the Colorado beetle is a dreaded potato pest. It is $\frac{3}{10}$ in. long, a little bigger than a ladybird. The convex, shiny back is longitudinally striped black and yellow, and the thorax, the region just behind the head, is spotted black and yellow. The specific name decemlineata *means ten-striped, as there are five black stripes on each wing-cover. The larva is equally conspicuous, orange-yellow with black markings on the head, black legs and three rows of black spots along each side. It has a characteristic hump-backed appearance.*

Potato pests

The Colorado beetle is a serious pest, feeding on potato leaves both as larva and adult, though it may occasionally resort to other plants of the potato family.

It passes the winter as a mature beetle, hibernating underground at a depth of 10–12 in. In late spring it comes out and, if it does not find itself surrounded by potato plants, flies in search of them, often for a distance of many miles. The female lays her eggs on the leaves, usually on the underside; they are yellow in colour and laid in batches. The larvae hatch in a few days, feed voraciously on the leaves and are fully grown in about 3 weeks. They then burrow into the soil to pupate, and a new generation of beetles emerges in 10–15 days. In Britain this second brood appears in late July or August, and if the weather stays warm a third generation may be produced. As soon as bad weather sets in, the beetles burrow into the soil and hibernate until the following spring.

The damage is done to the haulm, or above-ground part of the plant, which may be completely stripped of its leaves, so that the tubers cannot develop. The large number of eggs produced by each female and the rapid succession of generations are factors which make the Colorado beetle such a formidable pest. A single individual emerging in the spring may have thousands of descendants by the autumn.

33 insect enemies

The Colorado beetle seems to have no natural enemies that are effective in reducing its numbers. There are 33 different kinds of insects that prey on it, including bugs, beetles, wasps and flies, and one fly lays its eggs in the larvae of the Colorado beetle. Yet these account for only $\frac{1}{5}$ of the total. Spraying the potato foliage with an arsenical compound is the usual method of control. The important thing in Britain is to spot any infestation as early as possible and exterminate local populations before they have a chance to spread. Anyone who finds a Colorado beetle, either in a potato field or casually, should immediately report the matter at the nearest police station. The specimen *must* be taken along for its identity to be checked. This surveillance has so far proved effective in controlling the pest.

△ *In late spring a female Colorado beetle will lay a batch of yellow eggs on the potato leaf, which hatch in a few days.*

▽ *Fully-grown larva, about 3 weeks old. It is ready to burrow into the soil and pupate for about 15 days before emerging as an adult.*

An entomological curiosity

Like many insects which have become pests, the Colorado beetle is especially interesting. Almost all species of insects are conditioned to live in some particular type of climate. If the climate differs from that of their natural environment they will fail and die out at some stage in the life cycle. The Colorado beetle is a conspicuous exception to this rule. It can live the year round out of doors in Canada, where the winters are arctic in severity, in the hot deserts of Texas and Mexico and in our own cool wet climate. The beetle's habit of hibernating deep underground as an adult is probably the most important factor in promoting this quite unusual ability to adapt itself to any climate in which men can grow potatoes.

A potato bridge

Among the discoveries made in the Rocky Mountains by the American explorer Stephen Harriman Long, in the early 1820's, was a pretty black-and-yellow-striped beetle feeding on a sort of nightshade called buffalo burr *Solanum rostratum*. Neither it nor its food plant were particularly abundant, and it was simply an attractive insect living in a state of balance with its environment.

The buffalo burr is a member of the potato family. The potato is native to Peru and Ecuador, in South America. It was brought to Europe by the Spaniards and later found its way to the new colony of Virginia in North America. How this happened is not known. Neither Sir Walter Raleigh nor Sir Francis Drake, both of whom are credited with discovering it, took it there. In the course of the opening up and settlement of western America in the 1850's, potatoes were introduced and cultivated by the pioneers, and in Nebraska in 1859 it was found that the 'buffalo burr beetle' was turning its attention to the potato. Its numbers increased rapidly and it began to spread. No control measures were known at that time and the beetle spread from potato field to potato field, frequently destroying the whole crop. From Nebraska in 1859 it appeared in Illinois in 1864, in Ohio in 1869, and it reached the Atlantic coast in 1874. This indicates an average rate of travel of 85 miles a year. The potato fields of the United States had formed a bridge from west to east along which the beetle could travel. It also spread 400 miles northwards into Canada. The Atlantic formed a barrier, however, until 1922.

Then it was found in the Gironde region of France and from there it has extended its range all over continental Europe. It appeared in Tilbury in 1901, but the next outbreak in Britain was in Essex in 1933, where prompt control measures exterminated it. It has appeared from time to time in Britain since then, but has always been prevented from establishing itself. In 1946 there was a real danger it might become established. In 1947 infestations were discovered at 57 centres. In 1948 there were 11, and in 1949 not one was found. Prompt control measures had proved effective, much to the relief of the many British potato farmers.

G Hyde

class	Insecta
order	Coleoptera
family	Chrysomelidae
genus & species	*Leptinotarsa decemlineata*

Adults and larvae of the brightly-coloured Colorado beetle often live together on the same plant. Scourge of potato crops the world over, the Colorado beetle is an insect with an international price on its head, but if outbreaks are reported early, prompt control measures usually prove effective.

Coloration

When daylight falls on a white animal, the different parts of the light spectrum (all the wavelengths) are reflected, giving our eyes the impression of whiteness. When the animal is coloured, on the other hand, some of the wavelengths of the light falling on it are reflected whilst others are absorbed by the outer covering (hair, feathers, or hide) of the animal. So the colour of an animal is due to the removal by absorption of some of the wavelengths in the light incident on its external surface.

There are two principal methods by which wavelengths can be absorbed; by the physical nature of the reflecting surface, giving what are known as structural colours, or by pigments giving their own colours. In some cases an animal's colour is due to a combination of the two.

Structural colours

Structural colours are due either to interference or to the scattering of light. When a layer of oil spreads out on the surface of the water, interference colours can be seen: the colour of the oil changes with the angle of vision. The same effect can be seen in the iridescent feathers of a starling or humming-bird, and in certain beetles. The structure of an iridescent feather 'interferes' with the light striking it.

The other kind of structural colour, which does not change with the position of the observer's eye, is due to the scattering of light. The shorter waves in white light are scattered by extremely small particles. This kind of structural colour is responsible for the blue of the sky and the blue on a jay's wing; in neither case is a blue pigment present. In blue feathers the scattering units are actually minute air spaces in the solid keratin (the protein of which feathers are made). These are rather special cases, for most animal colours are due to the presence of chemical pigments.

Pigment colours

Perhaps the commonest animal pigment is melanin, which usually appears in the form of very insoluble granules. Melanin is made of various types of protein pigment; the colours presented depend on various conditions. It colours dark hair, fur, and skin, black feathers, black slugs and many other animals. The ink of octopus and cuttlefish is almost pure melanin. Sometimes melanin occurs in a brown or reddish-brown form and these colours can be seen in many mammals and in birds such as female pheasants.

Some of the brighter animal colours are produced by the pigments known as carotenoids which give red, orange and yellow colours. These pigments are of plant origin and they enter an animal's body in its food. The simplest is carotene, found in carrots. Most animals can join two molecules of carotene to make vitamin A. Carotenoids produce the reds and browns of sea-stars, the yellow of egg yolk and many other similar colours. A live lobster is blue; this colour is due to a combination of red carotenoid with a protein. When a lobster is boiled, the increase in heat causes the bond to break, leaving the red colour seen in a lobster offered for sale.

Food gives pink colour

The pink colour of flamingoes is due to another carotenoid which the bird obtains from its natural food. In zoos, flamingoes often lose their beautiful pink tone because they are fed on a diet lacking in carotenoid; the colour can be restored if the flamingoes are given food such as shrimps that contains carotenoid.

Melanins and carotenoids are very widespread in the animal kingdom, but some pigments have a very limited distribution. For instance, many sea-urchins have reddish or purplish colours which are due to naphthaquinone pigments. These are complicated organic compounds which are deposited in the hard spines and shell of the sea-urchin. The related anthraquinone pigments occur in some insects. The best known is cochineal, a red pigment in the body of the tropical American bug *Dactylopius cacti*. Cochineal is the basis of carmine which is used as a food colorant and watercolour pigment; it is also used in cosmetics, and the Aztecs dyed their cloth with it.

The pigment turacin has an even more restricted distribution, for it is found only in the red feathers of the turacos or Musophagidae, a family of tropical birds sometimes known as plantain-eaters. Turacin is a porphyrin combined with copper. Porphyrins without a metal occur in many other animals—some sea-stars, for example, molluscs, the shells of birds' eggs, and owl and bustard feathers—but here they do not contribute greatly to the coloration.

Tyrian purple is another rare pigment which is found only in a small gland in the dog-whelk *Nucella lapillus* and its relatives in the family Muricidae. In Roman times this pigment was extracted from the molluscs by boiling the whole animal. The resulting brew was used to dye the robes of emperors giving the colour known as imperial purple.

Not all the yellow, orange and red colours are produced by carotenoids. Some are due to pterins, such as xanthopterin, the yellow pigment of the brimstone butterfly. Pterins are also found in fishes, amphibians and reptiles; the pigment cells of goldfish contain both carotenoids and pterins.

Combined colours

Many animal colours are due to the combination of two or more pigments or of a pigment and a structural colour. A good example of the latter is the plumage of the tropical magpie *Cissa*, in which the feathers have a structure that scatters light overlaid by a layer of yellow pigment (probably carotenoid). The combination of a scattering structure (giving blue) and yellow pigment produces green feathers. When living in forests *Cissa* is usually green, but in open country this bird is blue, probably because the yellow pigment has been bleached in the light, leaving behind the blue structure.

The colours of animals can, therefore, be produced in many different ways and it is never wise to assume that one colour is always associated with one pigment. There is, in fact, much scope for further research into this interesting subject—with its inherent beauty as a bonus.

△ *Presence or absence of the pigment melanin dictates the whites, browns, and blacks of horses' hair.*
▷ *The feather structure of the peacock disrupts light waves, causing an iridescent sheen.*
▽ *Combination: the blue of the macaw is derived from light absorption by feather structure, the black from melanin pigment, and the white results from total reflection of all light waves.*

620

Protective coloration

All the colours of the rainbow can be seen in the millions of animal species. Many have coloured markings to identify themselves to their own kind, as in the guenon monkeys. In others the sexes have different colours, the male often being brilliantly coloured to attract a mate, as seen in the peacock or stickleback. In many species, however, the colours and patterns are to protect them.

A large number of animals are inconspicuous because their colours match the surroundings. This concealment or cryptic coloration is most effective and is often found in nature.

Some cicadas (bugs) of East Africa have colours and forms that closely resemble flowers. It is remarkable that they have the habit of bunching together, so looking like a floral inflorescence. One species has two coloured forms, a green and a yellow. These two morphs sit close together on vertical stems, with the green individuals at the top resembling buds and the yellow ones below looking like the opened flowers. This mimicry is so efficient that even experienced botanists have found themselves holding a bare stem after plucking a 'flower'.

Many animals with cryptic coloration, especially insects, have a second line of defence if attacked. Some moths and butterflies have eye-spots, looking like big vertebrate eyes, which are suddenly exposed by moving the second pair of wings. The eyed hawk moth will perform this beautifully for anyone who gives it a 'dig' when it is at rest. These huge eyes cause any small bird to flee immediately. Some moths, cryptic at rest, expose bright markings rather than eye-spots when disturbed which leaves the attacker confused as the moth becomes conspicuous one second and then disappears the next. When one studies a zebra it is hard to find a reason why it has such a flashy pyjama suit (below). It baffles scientists even today and several views are held. In the shade of a tree a zebra's dramatic stripes do give concealment. Close to a zebra herd, the stripes break up the animal's outline so a predator, such as a lion, cannot tell where one zebra ends and the next begins. When he springs to attack his judgement may be wrong and the zebra has time to escape. This is known as disruptive coloration. Another view is that the stripes exaggerate the size of the animal so again the attacker may miss when he jumps. Many animals accentuate their conspicuousness by being brightly coloured as seen in coral snakes, gila monsters and caterpillars (opposite). Again, this is subject to imitation. Many harmless moths derive protection from looking like inedible species, and only the experienced can tell true from false coral snakes.

Aligned confusion: a zebra's stripes probably serve to break up the body outline, making it difficult for a predator to focus on a single individual.

KH Stanley

Disrupt to disguise: the garden carpet moth (right) **Xanthroe fluctuata** *shows the concealment effect of a disruptive pattern, having some parts which blend in with the background, while others differ strongly from it. The gecko (below) combines cryptic and disruptive coloration to help disguise itself against the tree trunk. Another means of defence is that it can shed its tail (by a process called autotomy) when it is attacked and so escape capture.*

Blend and bluff: many animals gain protection by imitating their surroundings. The angle shades moth **Phlogophora meticulosa** *(below) with folded wings, head crest and mottled patterns gives excellent concealment among dead leaves. Many insects such as grasshoppers, moths and stick insects have adapted to resemble growing twigs. The New Zealand prickly stick insect* **Acanthoxyla prasina** *(right) shows a cryptic coloration resting attitude on a bramble bush.*

Peter Ward

PH Ward

Eat me at your peril: the bright colours of the spurge moth caterpillar (below) warn predators that it is unpalatable. Warning patterns of animals include red, yellow, black and white — all colours that stand out well. All are used to good effect in this handsome specimen. On a fern frond, bird dropping or spider? A crab spider successfully mimics a bird dropping (below right). This technique is unusual; most crab spider species match to perfection the flowers on which they lurk.

GS Giacomelli

MPL Fooden

623

Poisonous butterflies and moths

The fact that butterflies and moths (Lepidoptera) may contain poisonous substances in their body tissues is a relatively new discovery. Only ten years ago Karl Jordan, one of the greatest entomologists of his time, commenting on this possibility, wrote authoritatively: 'The garden tiger moth, in its adult stage, is a completely harmless insect.' It is now known that this moth (*Arctia caja* L.) secretes a toxic substance ($\beta\beta$ dimethylacrylylcholine) in its defensive glands; that the burnet moths and foresters (Zygaenids) release cyanide (HCN) from their body tissues when crushed; that the cinnabar moth (*Callimorpha jacobaeae* L.) contains poisonous alkaloids (senecio alkaloids) plus a heavy concentration of histamine; the monarch butterfly (*Danaus plexippus* L.) stores heart poisons (cardenolides) in its haemolymph (blood); and that certain swallowtail butterflies (*Papilio*) ingest and store a poisonous acid (aristolochic acid) in their bodies.

Butterflies and moths have many enemies. They are attacked on the wing, for instance, by birds, bats, hornets, robberflies, dragonflies and other large insects, and when at rest, by birds, monkeys, lemurs, mice and various other small mammals, mantids and similar insects.

The poisonous substances in their bodies are part of their defence mechanisms – they produce a repellent taste or vile smell (or both) and local irritation of the mucous membranes of the predator, or if ingested may cause severe pain or discomfort after they have been swallowed. Thus, for example, a jay vomits violently about 10 – 15 minutes after swallowing the monarch butterfly. This is because the heart poisons in the body tissues of the butterfly also act upon the stomach, causing contraction of smooth muscle and the regurgitation of the meal. Two monarch butterflies contain enough heart poisons, if retained by the bird, to kill a starling.

Warning coloration

Bright colours and warning coloration are often associated with defence mechanisms of these types. Thus butterflies and moths armed with chemical repellents are often extremely conspicuous both in appearance and behaviour. If an inexperienced predator captures such a specimen it will receive a sharp lesson. It will associate these disagreeable qualities with the brilliant colour of the insect and in future keep at a safe distance. Expressed differently, it pays these insects to advertise their presence and the first victim is sacrificed for the future protection of the population.

The great naturalists of the 19th century had observed that a number of species of butterflies which were avoided by bird predators fed on poisonous plants, and deduced correctly that some of their repellent qualities were derived from their larval food. Thus certain swallowtails feed on birthwort and its allies (*Aristolochia*) and the monarch butterfly and its relatives on the poisonous milkweeds (*Asclepias*).

In the course of time they have evolved a

△ *Only in recent years have certain butterflies and moths been found to contain poisonous substances. The two monarch butterflies seen above store enough heart poisons (cardenolides) to kill a starling.*

PH Ward

method of extracting and storing these toxins and using them for their own protection. Their relationship with poisonous plants, however, involves another probably more important aspect. Eggs and young larvae laid or hatching on such foliage avoid destruction because the large herbivores do not feed upon these poisonous plants. Even hungry camels in the desert avoid *Asclepias*. The burnet moth larvae which feed on clovers and vetches that contain cyanide are thus protected from grazing rabbits, which are known to avoid these strains of the plants. The period in an insect's life when natural selection acts most severely is in the very early stages. Hundreds of eggs may be laid by one moth but the majority of the caterpillars hatching from them die when they are still tiny. An immense advantage must be conferred on a species with a food supply so noxious that other animals avoid it, and which consequently not only has more to eat, but is not itself accidentally eaten by grazing herbivores. It is obvious that once a species has evolved a strain that can eat such a plant it will probably leave more living offspring than other strains. The next steps, that is the ability to store the toxic substances and carry them over to the adult insect, are additional advantages which may evolve with time. This in turn leads on to warning coloration and the warning way of life.

Poison paradoxes

It should, however, be clearly understood that all Lepidoptera with chemical defence mechanisms do not get their poisons directly from their food plants. Some of these toxic substances are synthesised by the insects themselves. The garden tiger is a good example of this. It is a curious fact that the toxic substance found in its defence glands has only once previously been identified in a living animal; on this occasion it was found in the poison glands of a marine snail. Furthermore, all insects living on poisonous plants do not store toxins in their bodies. A large number, for example, feed on tobacco and presumably obtain indirect protection by this means, but nicotine is apparently too deadly a poison to store in living tissues and the examples so far examined among tobacco feeders either excrete the poisons rapidly or change them within their bodies into less toxic substances. In such cases the insects concerned are not warningly coloured. However, here again one cannot generalise, for although most insects with poisons in their tissues are brightly coloured, some very toxic night-flying moths have concealing coloration, and almost certainly prove fatal to any unsuspecting animal that consumes them.

Harmless mimic the harmful

Again there are some warningly coloured butterflies which are quite innocuous in reality, but deceitfully resemble (or mimic) those which have chemical defence mechanisms – sheep in wolves' clothing – and thereby gain protection from predators which mistake them for dangerous species. This does not appear to be common among the Lepidoptera of Europe but it is widespread in certain tropical countries. The hornet clearwing of Europe is one example since it looks like a hornet and bears little resemblance to a moth.

The investigation of poisons in insects is rather a difficult matter, since they are present in small quantities and require complicated and time-consuming techniques for their identification. Probably, when more is known about the subject, it will be found that many warningly coloured insects which feed on poisonous plants and can store the toxins in their food have simultaneously evolved the mechanism for secreting additional poisons themselves, or at any rate substances which boost the effect of the main chemical deterrent.

Common dolphin

Smaller than the bottlenosed dolphin, the common dolphin is up to 8 ft long and weighs up to 165 lb. The beak is narrow and sharply cut off from the forehead. The jaws have 40-44 teeth on each side of the upper and lower jaws. The dolphin is black, sometimes with brown or violet and light spots above and white below. A dark stripe runs from eye to snout. Around Malaya and neighbouring islands, common dolphins may frequently be dark grey.

There are several other species in the same genus as the common dolphin. Dolphins of the genus Delphinus *are found between New Guinea and Australia, from South Africa across the Indian Ocean and all along the West Pacific to Japan.*

Range and habits

Common dolphins are found in the tropical and temperate seas, never going as far north or south as the bottlenose dolphin.

Off Europe, they never go farther north than Iceland and Finmark (northern Norway). They appear to be migratory. For instance, schools of common dolphins can be seen in Algerian waters in summer, but they disappear in winter. In other species migration is related to the movements of the fish on which they feed, and this could well be the case for common dolphins.

Many aspects of the common dolphin's habits, life history and physiology are very similar to those described for the bottlenose dolphins. Their diving and swimming mechanisms are very much alike, but common dolphins cannot stay submerged so long. The usual length of a dive is 2–3 minutes and they are reported to die if

kept under for 5 minutes. Common dolphins are among the fastest cetaceans. While they may cruise at about 5 knots, they can swim at 20 knots (24 mph) for a considerable length of time. Faster speeds have been recorded with dolphins swimming in ships' bow-waves, when they hold their bodies at an angle, using them as surf boards.

Common dolphins travel in schools which, as in the bottlenose dolphins, are made up of both sexes and all ages. There is no leader but males bear the scars of fights with each other. The schools are often very large, and in the Black Sea a school of 10 000 was reported. Schools as large as this must be very rare and probably form only where there are even vaster concentrations of fish.

Playing schools

It is not unusual to see a school of dolphins or porpoises playing, and the common dol-

phin seems to be the most playful species. A school can be watched from a ship or cliff for an hour or more without the dolphins travelling out of sight. Their behaviour certainly appears to be playing just for the fun of it, rather than for a strictly useful purpose as is most behaviour. When dolphins are swimming normally, they follow an undulating path, continually rising to come to the surface to breathe.

Usually only the top of the head breaks surface, but in the simplest form of play the dolphins exaggerate the rise and fall so that they leap out of the water, curving over in an arc to fall back into the water.

Other games are played, in which the dolphins leap out vertically and land on back, belly or side in a 'belly flop', or they will roll over and over or swim on their backs. Another trick is to swim at the surface, raising the tail and bringing it down on the water with a loud smack every 2 or 3 seconds.

It is an impressive sight to watch dolphins playing and it is made all the more so by the way the dolphins join together to play. One moment they are swimming in a line, then one leaps into the air and a second later all have bunched together, rolling, twisting and splashing, several of them often leaping out in a perfect line-abreast formation.

Feeding

The food—fish, squid and cuttlefish—is the same general diet as that of other dolphins. Flying fish and other species that live near the surface are taken.

Mother helps baby dolphin

Again, the breeding habits of the common dolphin are very similar to those described for the bottlenose dolphin. The calf is born tailfirst and the mother helps it to the surface to take its first breath. If it is injured she will support it until it dies. Suckling takes place underwater and milk is forced into the calf's mouth by the contraction of muscles around the mammary gland.

The calves are born from midwinter to summer after a gestation of 9 months.

The tourist trap at Hippo

References to dolphins are frequent in classical literature, and they appear regularly on Greek and Roman coins and mosaics. The stories connected with them are usually of their relationships with man, often aiding someone in distress. Arion of Lesbos, for instance, was saved by dolphins. He was on his way back from a music competition in Sicily, when his shipmates, jealous of his prowess at singing and poetry and envious of the valuable prizes he had won, conspired to throw him overboard. Arion picked up his cithara, the instrument on which his fame was based, and played so sweetly that a school of dolphins came to listen. Then, before his enemies could bind him he leapt overboard and was carried to safety on the back of one of the dolphins.

Another story that was thought to be as mythical as that of Arion is the account by the Roman naturalist Pliny of the dolphin of Hippo. Hippo was a North African port and the boys there had a sport in which they allowed themselves to be carried out to sea by the river that ran into the sea there. He who went farthest was the winner. One day one of the boys found a dolphin playing about him, swimming around and, eventually, under him to lift him onto its back. The story of this incident got around the town and crowds flocked to see the dolphin who became very tame, allowing people to swim around and pat it, but only giving rides to the boy it first befriended.

This story was treated as a fable until in 1955 a bottlenose dolphin appeared off the New Zealand town of Opononi. 'Opo', as this dolphin was called, also gave rides. The story of the dolphin of Hippo ended sadly. The townspeople of Hippo became tired of acting as hosts to all the visitors who flocked to see their famous dolphin and it was secretly harpooned. How times have changed, that a centre of tourism should deliberately destroy its chief attraction to regain peace and quiet!

class	**Mammalia**
order	**Cetacea**
family	**Delphinidae**
genus & species	***Delphinus delphis***

△ *Common dolphins explode from the glass-clear waters of Cook Strait, between the North and South Islands of New Zealand. Unlike bottlenose dolphins, common dolphins do not take kindly to captivity and are not easily tamed. They travel in schools, made up of both sexes and all ages.*

Common dolphin *(Delphinus delphinus)*

Common dolphins are found in tropical and temperate seas but never go as far north or south as the bottlenose dolphin

Common dolphin: sleek, graceful acrobat of the sea

◁ *Dolphin fresco in the 'Queen's Megaron' or hall at Knossos, Crete. Sea life was a favourite subject with the artists of the Minoan culture in Crete—and with the later Greeks. The dolphin was an emblem of the Greek city of Corinth.*

▷ *A dolphin's speed and agility in water enable it to catch fish, squid and cuttlefish as food. Its many sharp teeth help prevent their escape before being swallowed.*

▽ *Left. Birth of a dolphin. Since bottlenose dolphins thrive in seaquaria (see p. 408), remarkable details like this can be observed.*

▽ *Right: A surfacing dolphin takes a deep breath through its blowhole, which is done every few minutes. Like all whales, the dolphin's blowhole on the top of the head is a specialised nostril; when whales 'spout', they are snorting out the used air.*

Graham Pizzey NHPA

Popperfoto

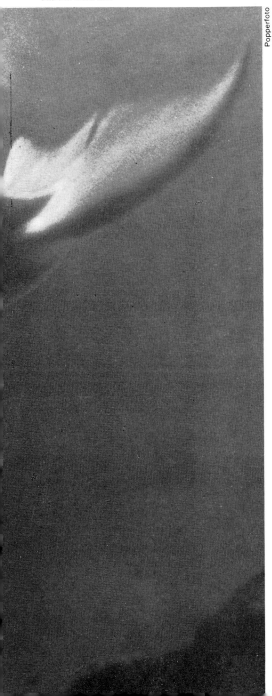

Marineland. Florida

Roy A Harris and KR Duff

Frogspawn jelly sticks together and protects the eggs, and perhaps prevents attacks by bacteria and fungi.

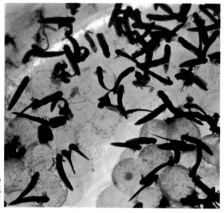

P Morris

On emerging, the tadpoles attach themselves to the jelly but do not feed, breathing through three pairs of external gills.

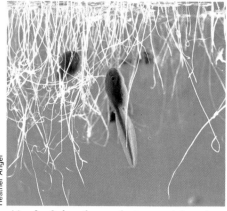

Heather Angel

After 2—3 days the mouth opens and the tadpoles begin to feed off weed and algae. External gills vanish in 3 weeks.

Common frog

The common frog of Europe could be called the laboratory frog, because, in the British Isles at least, this is the frog dissected by every biology student. Its colour is variable, usually green, but the ground colour may be grey, yellow, brown, orange or red. Red frogs are particularly common in Scotland. Certain markings, however, are consistent. There are dark transverse bars on the hindlegs, a streak on the forearm and in front of the eye and a brown patch behind each eye. Other marks include speckles, spots and marbling. The underparts are usually lighter, dirty white or pale yellow in males and yellow or orange in females. The overall colouring can vary to some extent according to light conditions.

The skin is smooth with many small wart-like slime or mucous glands. These keep the skin moist while the frog is out of water. This is important as frogs lose water through their skins very easily and a layer of moisture also allows them to absorb oxygen through the skin. In the breeding season the male's skin becomes more slimy and the warts on the females become larger and pearly white.

The common frog's distribution covers most of Europe and Asia north of the tropical regions. It is found all over the British Isles except the Outer Hebrides, Orkney and Shetland. It was probably introduced to Ireland and is now found in about half the counties. It is usually only seen during the breeding season when large numbers may be seen gathering in ponds to mate and spawn. The assertion that 'any pond will do' for spawning is not strictly correct. It is based on the fact that they will sometimes spawn in ruts in cart-tracks which dry up before the eggs even hatch. Normally they prefer shallow water a few inches deep, but will spawn in 3 ft or more. Furthermore, certain ponds may contain spawn every year while others less than 100 yd away never do. Why some should be preferred to others is not clear, but an individual frog will return each year to the same pond, and newly built-up areas are sometimes invaded by frogs looking for ponds that are now filled in. This together with the infilling of ponds by farmers is probably one of the main reasons for the decline of frogs in Britain. Another major factor, however, is the heavy toll taken by school biology classes. Some British commercial frog suppliers are even getting frogs from Holland or breeding them themselves.

Outside the breeding season the frogs live a solitary life on land, usually in damp places, near ponds and marshes but they can be found some distance from water squatting among grass. In Germany they are called grass frogs. In October or later — the exact time depends on the weather — common frogs go into hibernation, or rather torpor, for they will become active on mild days, hopping about in search of food. The date they come out of hibernation again depends on the weather. In southwest England they spawn from the beginning of February. In the north of Scotland spawning will take place later.

Amphibian insectivores

As would be expected, frogs live on the small animals around them. Their favourite food animals are slugs and snails, followed by beetles, caterpillars and woodlice. Many other insects, and spiders, centipedes and mites, are eaten. When they are in water, the frogs eat small freshwater crustaceans. They do not hunt their prey, but lie in wait and catch passing animals with their extensible tongues.

Tadpoles feed on organisms ranging from bacteria to small crustaceans such as daphnia, including single-celled algae and amoebae. They also scrape algae off water plants with horny mandibles, and lip teeth. The food and water are swept into the gullet by currents set up by cilia and strained off, the water passing out through the gill clefts and the spiracle.

A frog's embrace

Shortly after coming out of hibernation, frogs make their way back to the ponds. It has been suggested that they are guided to water by the smell of the algae, essential for the tadpoles' growth, growing there, but the arrival of frogs at filled-in ponds would disprove this. There is evidence that frogs and toads navigate by the sun or stars.

The male frogs arrive first with the females arriving a little later. Sometimes they wait there a week or more before spawning, but another time the spawning will be finished in a couple of days. The males croak, mainly during the day. Compared with some other frogs and toads, common frogs are very quiet. Croaking is produced by passing air backwards and forwards across the vocal chords from lungs to mouth. The mouth is not opened, so frogs can croak while under water. While croaking, the throat is distended under the chin.

During the spawning period males will

Frogs amid spawn. Mating occurs in spring, usually March, when frogs leave their winter quarters.

W Harstrick: Bavaria

By 8 weeks the hind legs are fully developed. The broad transparent webbed tail propels the tadpole in a slow, fish-like motion.

At 3 months the front legs break through the operculum covering the gills. The tail shortens and starts to become absorbed into the body.

Final product: young frogs. The skin has been shed, taking with it the larval lips and horny jaws, leaving a much wider mouth.

attempt to embrace any object in amplexus, wrapping the front legs around it and holding on with a vice-like grip aided by the special swellings which develop on their hands at this time. Sometimes fish are drowned because a frog has grasped them round the gills. If one male clasps another, the latter grunts to show the former its mistake. Males can also recognise gravid females by the roughness of the skin they develop and their size. Amplexus lasts about a day and a male may mate with several females.

Each female lays 1—2 thousand eggs, which are suddenly ejected in a period of less than 5 seconds. The male sheds his sperm over them immediately afterwards, then the pair disengage.

At first the eggs are $\frac{1}{10}$ in. diameter and they sink to the bottom of the pool, but the jelly surrounding them swells up and they become buoyant, floating to the surface in the familiar masses of frogspawn. The jelly is not used as food but as a protection against enemies and against cold. When the surrounding water is freezing, frogspawn is a degree or so warmer because the black egg absorbs radiant heat from the sun which is trapped by the jelly.

From tadpole to frog

In about 2 weeks the tadpoles have developed. The egg membrane is then dissolved or digested by a special gland. After emerging each tadpole clings to the remains

of the jelly mass with special adhesive organs. At this stage it has external gills, no limbs and the head, body and tail are merged together like a fish. Later, the external gills disappear, the mouth opens and the tadpole begins to feed, while the internal gills develop from buds on the sides of the head. The gills are covered by a flap of skin, the operculum. Later, the limbs grow, the hindlegs appearing first as the forelegs are covered by the operculum. Finally, the outer skin is cast, the gills are absorbed as the lungs come into action and the tail is absorbed into the body, resulting in a fully-formed froglet. The froglets, measuring $\frac{1}{2}$ in., move to the edge of the pool until their legs strengthen and they leap out into the grass and disperse. In mountain districts tadpoles sometimes overwinter, maturing the next spring.

By their first winter the froglets measure 1 in., and they become sexually mature at 3 years. In captivity common frogs have lived for 12 years.

Many enemies

Common frogs have many enemies. To list the animals that eat them would almost list the British flesh-eating animals. Apart from the carnivorous mammals and predatory birds, hedgehogs, gulls and crows eat frogs. Their main enemies are probably grass snakes and herons.

Tadpoles are eaten by fish and by invertebrates such as water beetle and dragonfly

larvae. When frightened adult frogs escape by leaping away.

Raining frogs and fishes

Every now and then there is a story in the newspapers about a storm bringing not only rain, but showers of animals. The Romans recorded rains of fishes. On the 17th August, 1921, the streets of North London were carpeted with little frogs, and other parts of the world have been showered with toads, crabs, worms, mice and winkles. The explanation for some of these phenomena is that the animals were lifted by a whirlwind or waterspout and carried up to the clouds and deposited, some distance away, with rain.

Rains of frogs have been reported more often than of other animals but this is because of the behaviour of the young frogs. As we have seen, the froglets wait in the shadows of the pools, and heavy rain might occur at the same time as their emergence. In the days before the filling-in of ponds and their pollution this was a spectacular sight, for the ground became alive with frogs. This naturally led people to think that they had arrived with the rain, but less credulous and more observant people noticed that they were coming from ponds, discredited the idea and went on to affirm that this was the basis for all stories of rains of frogs.

Another strange form of 'precipitation' is the Star-Slime or Rot of the Stars, a whitish jelly-like substance that used to be found lying on the ground, especially in the autumn. This was investigated by a zoologist in 1926. He found it was the remains of some glands in the reproductive system of female frogs. The frogs had been eaten in vast numbers by various animals, but the glands had passed through undigested. Then, becoming wet, the jelly in the glands swelled up and burst to leave a slimy mess that did not decompose easily.

Self-service: trapped on the frog's sticky tongue, the worm will be swallowed whole.

class	**Amphibia**
order	**Salientia**
family	**Ranidae**
genus & species	*Rana temporaria*

G Kinns

Jane Burton: Photo Res

△ *Common frog in defence posture. A frightened frog may inflate its body, put its hands over its eyes, and draw its hindlegs against its body. This could make it harder for an enemy to grip.*

△ *Albino common frog. The value of pigmentation lies in protective coloration and protection from excessive light. This version would probably be easy meat for predators.*

▽ *The common frog's smooth skin contains many small slime or mucous glands. These keep the skin moist while the frog is out of water, since water is very easily lost through the skin.*

JAL Cooke

Common rat

The terms 'black rat' and 'brown rat', commonly used to distinguish the two species, are liable to cause confusion because both have a wide range of coloration, so that a black rat may appear brown, and vice versa. It is becoming the practice now to speak of them as the ship rat and the common rat. The common rat is considerably larger than the ship rat, averaging $9\frac{1}{4}$ in. from nose to the base of the tail and weighing up to 1 lb. In comparison with the ship rat, the common rat has smaller ears, a proportionately shorter and fatter tail and shaggier fur.

The white rats used in laboratories are specially bred albino varieties of common rats.

Man's camp followers

The lives of common rats are closely bound with man. They share his buildings and food, attacking his crops both before they are harvested and when they are in the warehouses. They have followed foodstuffs aboard ships, and the ships have carried rats around the world. Now, common rats are to be found from Alaska, where they are known to suffer from frostbite, to the whaling stations of South Georgia, on the fringes of the Antarctic.

The origins of the common rat are rather obscure. It is thought that it spread across Europe from central Asia, and at one time it was suggested that it arrived in England on board ships coming from Norway at the beginning of the 18th century. For this reason it became known as the Norway or Hanover rat. The allusion to the Hanoverian kings, who arrived at much the same time, appears to have been a political joke. The current theory is that common rats arrived in ships trading with the East between 1728 and 1730. At the same time they were spreading overland across Europe. In 1727 vast hordes were seen crossing the Volga. Millions perished in the crossing but there were enough survivors to make nothing safe in the houses on the other side.

Rats on the march

Swarms of rats on the march were often reported at this time and would, no doubt, still be reported if it were not for vigorous control campaigns. Even now, however, there are sporadic reports of rat migrations when local populations build up to plague proportions. Eye witnesses speak of 'phalanxes' or 'columns' of rats. One column crossing a road was several yards wide and took half an hour to pass. Observers speak of strange whistling and chirruping noises as the rats call to each other, and one man recalled how, as a child, he saw such a column with a rearguard of very young rats, old mangy rats, blind rats and crippled rats, accompanied by others which appeared to be helping their weaker companions.

The trouble with these stories is that details are usually imprecise. Often they are told only at secondhand or are recalled from childhood memories. All that can be said is that rats will migrate *en masse* when their original home becomes overcrowded. This habit they share with other rodents, the most famous example being the mass movements of the Scandinavian lemmings.

When they have no migratory urge rats keep to a fairly restricted home range in warehouses, farm buildings, corn ricks, rubbish tips, hedgerows and woodlands. They are often found along river banks and, being good swimmers, they are sometimes mistaken for water voles.

The home range, or territory, is inhabited by a family group that live amicably together, with little fighting except by females defending their nests. Strange rats are not tolerated and there are border skirmishes where territories meet. If a strange male is placed in a colony of captive rats, where it cannot escape, it is usually dead within a few hours.

Within the home range there is a system of runs, regularly used by the rats as they go about foraging. These are often underground, and when above ground they are built to take advantage of natural cover, for the runs give protection from enemies and as the rats come to know every inch of the way they can bolt along them at full speed when danger threatens.

Destructive feeders

Common rats feed on an incredible assortment of foods, and because of the versatility of their feeding habits and the enormous numbers which rat populations reach they are extremely destructive. At one time they were beneficial to some extent, acting as scavengers, but as hygiene has improved rats have become mere parasites.

Their main food is grain, either in fields or in stores. They will also attack root crops, and are a serious pest of sugar beet in East Anglia. Rats eat more flesh than most rodents and, where they live in meat stores, they eat little else. All manner of animals are captured; the remains of house mice, the skins turned inside out, are often found near rats' nests. They will attack poultry runs, often carrying eggs away to their burrows, and even ducklings are not safe because common rats are expert at swimming and diving.

Prolific breeders

There is little or no courtship before mating and a bond never forms between the pair. The female builds a spherical nest, of any material available, where the litter is born after a gestation of about 24 days. The young, 4–10 in number depending on conditions such as age and social position of mother, are born naked and helpless. Their

The life of the common rat is closely linked with man; it shares his buildings and food, attacking his crops both before they are harvested and when they are stored. It is thought to have originated in Asia and has become worldwide, often taken by ships to new countries.

G Kinns AFA

eyes and ears open a few days later and they leave the nest when 3 weeks old.

When the home range is in an environment that alters little throughout the year, like a wheat rick, breeding takes place all the time. This does not mean that each female breeds all the year round, for each produces only 3–5 litters a year, but there are always some females in breeding condition. In fields and hedgerows there are one or two annual peaks of breeding.

A female rat begins breeding when about 80 days old and can then produce anything up to 50 young a year. This figure is never reached in practice because mortality, especially of young rats, becomes very high when the population is large. As many as 99% will die before they are adults, and most adults do not live for more than a year. This very rapid rate of reproduction and turnover means that rats are very difficult to control. With such a high natural mor-

Jane Burton: Photo Res

△*Typical brown rat litter, containing 16 2-day-old babies: naked, helpless — but future vermin.*

▷ *Rats at home in a ruined cellar. They can usually thrive on any food they can get.*

Jane Burton: Photo Res

△ *The rat is an efficient swimmer, paddling with its feet — as this specimen demonstrates.*

▽ *The Pied Piper nursery legend — glamour for the grisly work of the rodent exterminator.*

Mansell

tality even a very determined onslaught with poison and traps will have very little lasting effect on the numbers. They will only remove rats which are shortly going to die anyway.

Many enemies

Tawny owls, stoats, weasels and foxes all hunt rats, although even a champion killer like a stoat may have difficulty killing a healthy full-grown rat. Since the myxomatosis epidemic killed off rabbits in 1953, foxes have eaten many more rats.

Around farmyards, cats account for a good few rats, and it has been shown that, although cats cannot reduce the population of rats on their own, if the population is reduced by poisoning, the cats can prevent the rats from regaining their numbers.

How do rats carry eggs?

Egg-stealing is a well-known habit of rats. If one keeps poultry it is not unusual to come across an egg when digging in the garden some distance from the hen run. A closer examination shows that it was lying in a rat's burrow. How does a rat move such an awkward thing as an egg? A story often recounted is of one rat lying on its back, clutching the egg, while another drags it along by the tail, or an ear or leg. This sounds a most improbable story but a considerable number of intelligent people are sure they have seen it happen. A rat-catcher once described how he opened the door of a shed and saw a rat scuttle away from what appeared to be a piece of sacking with an egg lying on it. To his surprise the 'sacking' got up and ran away. It was another rat, so the rat-catcher assumed that he had caught two rats in the act of co-operating to carry an egg.

Unfortunately, this sort of observation cannot be repeated to order. Rats are very wary and will shun a place if they realise anyone is watching, and sprinkling flour or chalk around eggs to see if a tell-tale trail shows that a rat has been dragged on its back has never produced results. It may be, however, that the answer is less exciting but none the less interesting. Rats have also been seen bounding along with an egg in the forepaws. This again seems a little improbable but it has been observed in a few other rodents, and it does not assume a high degree of co-operation between two rats. If it then happened that the rat met another their subsequent behaviour might well give the impression of such co-operation. For when two rats of the same family group meet one falls on its back in a submissive posture, while the other licks it. Suppose a rat carrying an egg in its forepaws had met another and rolled on to its back, still clutching its egg, when someone disturbed them. In the split second before they bolted for cover it might look as if the rat grooming the recumbent one had in fact been dragging it along.

class	**Mammalia**
order	**Rodentia**
family	**Muridae**
genus & species	***Rattus norvegicus***

Common seal

Known as the harbor seal in the United States, this is a true seal — that is, the hind flippers trail behind it and cannot be tucked forward under the body as in a sea lion. This means that the common seal can only crawl overland. Although they move on their bellies with the assistance of the foreflippers, common seals can move surprisingly fast when in a hurry, especially down a smooth, sloping sand bank. Common seals belong to the group of earless seals, in contrast to the eared seals, although they do have very small external ear 'flaps' which are usually concealed in the ear opening.

Male common seals are 5—6 ft long and females 4—5 ft, with a short tail of 3 or 4 in. hidden between the rear flippers. The coat of short coarse hair varies in colour from silver and grey to brown and almost black. Light coats are spotted and blotched with dark markings, and dark coats with light markings. The usual colour is light grey marked with black, lighter on the undersides.

In northern seas

Common seals are found around the shores of the northern oceans. Off Europe, they are found along the western shores as far south as East Anglia and Holland, into the Baltic Sea as far as Stockholm and north to the North Cape of Norway. On the eastern seaboard of America they reach Maine and extend as far north as Ellesmere Island. They occur on both sides of the Pacific Ocean, reaching Lower California and Korea.

In Britain, there are breeding colonies in the Shetland and Orkney Islands, the Dornoch and Moray Firths, the west coast and outer Hebrides and on Scroby Sands off Norfolk. The Irish population breeds in the counties of Londonderry, Antrim and Down. Common seals are also seen on other parts of the coast and sometimes go up rivers. They have been seen near Arundel in Sussex and at Teddington on the River Thames, upstream from London.

Common seals are found in sheltered places in deep sea lochs, or on rocky coasts where archipelagos of small islands and skerries provide shelter. The Wash of eastern England houses 6,500 common seals, the largest population in Europe.

Feeding on the sea bed

The main food of seals is fish, and the diet of the common seal is no exception. Most of the fish they eat live on the sea bed, such as flatfish, gobies, soles and sand eels. They also eat prawns, crabs, cockles and whelks. More active species are caught, including mackerel, trout, salmon and squid.

Once weaned, the young seals are mainly shrimp-eaters, then during their first winter they add fish, crabs and molluscs to their diet. Adults are mainly fish eaters but the diet varies in different localities. The fact that they will eat sea-trout and salmon has

RW Vaughan

◁ *Common seal colonies are found along quiet shores of the northern oceans.*

△ *Young common seal. The slit behind the eye is the external opening of the ear.*

Beringer and Pampaluchi: Bavaria

△*Seals are able to close their nostrils when diving, so preventing water entering the lungs.*

▽ *A seal's whiskers or vibrissae pick up vibrations, helping in the tracking of prey.*

G Kinns AFA

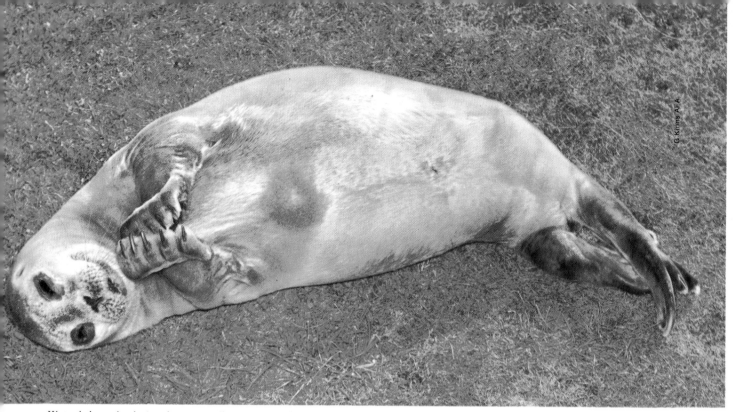

Water baby on land. A seal cannot walk with its back flippers, as these cannot bend forward; but it can use its front flippers to crawl overland on its belly.

made common seals unpopular with fishermen. Some learn that an easy meal is to be had by robbing nets. Unfortunately they do a disproportionate amount of damage by injuring and leaving more fish than they eat, and the younger seals sometimes get caught in the nets, which are torn as they wrench themselves clear.

Water babies

The pups are born in June and July, when the females gather in shallow and sheltered coves. The pups are born on sandbanks or tide-covered rocks between one high tide and another. For this to be possible, birth must be rapid and the newborn pup must be in a sufficiently advanced state to be able to swim almost immediately. Most seal pups are born with a fluffy coat of fur called the lanugo, which is shed before they take to the water. The pups of common seals lose their lanugo, which is white, just before they are born, or sometimes just after. Thus they are born with the adult coat, a necessary adaptation, as they must be able to swim immediately. It sometimes happens that there is a strong swell and a high tide in the breeding cove, and the pups are born without harm while the mothers are in the water.

For the first few days of their lives the pups rarely come ashore. They spend their time floating in the water near the shore with their mothers in close attendance, often touching them. Within 2 days they can swim and dive in the shallow water, sometimes being assisted by their mothers, who shepherd them with their foreflippers. Later they can come on land, the initial landing sometimes being made on the mothers' backs. Suckling takes place for 4 weeks, during which time the pup grows its teeth, puts on a layer of blubber and begins to learn how to look after itself. It is then abandoned and the mother leaves to moult and then mate. Gestation takes 9 months be-

cause there is delayed implantation (see armadillo p 83), the embryo not starting to develop until autumn.

Clubbed for their fur

Killer whales and polar bears are the main danger to common seals, although in many parts they are shot or clubbed, either as pups for their fur, or as adults because of the damage to fishing nets. Common seals are very wary of man, taking to the sea at the slightest disturbance.

A woolly birthday suit

The soft fluffy fur with which most baby seals are born lacks the coarse guard hairs of the adult pelage. This coat is moulted and replaced by the adult coat before the pups take to the water. The pups of seals living in the Arctic have white coats, which are much sought after by hunters, but it is not known whether they are white to reduce heat loss in the cold atmosphere or to prevent enemies seeing them against the ice and snow. There are objections to both theories and there may be a totally different reason.

Common seals are different, their pup coat, or lanugo, is shed before they are

born or just afterwards, and this is probably because they have to take to the water just a few hours after birth. One population of common seals, however, behaves like other seals. From the Bering Sea to Korea common seals breed slightly earlier, from February to April, and the pups are born on ice floes where they stay for 2 or 3 weeks. Like the other Arctic seals, these common seal pups have a fluffy white coat which is moulted just before they enter the water.

In 1988, more than 16,000 dead seals were washed up on the beaches around the North Sea. Between 50% and 70% of the common seals in the North Sea died. The primary cause of these deaths is thought to be a previously undescribed virus. The origin of the disease remains unknown but may be linked to the increasing pollution of the North Sea, which has caused many other ecological disasters.

class	**Mammalia**
order	**Pinnipedia**
family	**Phocidae**
genus & species	*Phoca vitulina*

Common seals are found around the shores of the northern oceans where they feed on seabed fish.

Common seal *(Phoca vitulina)*

Common toads mating.

Common toad

Despite a superficial resemblance to the common frog, few people have difficulty in recognising a common toad, even if they recoil in horror on seeing it. It has a flatter back and relatively shorter legs. Instead of the moist, bright skin of the frog, the toad has a dull, wrinkled, pimply skin. Its movements are slow and grovelling, and, although it can jump a short distance on all fours, it usually walks laboriously over the ground.

The rough skin blends well with the earth, so a toad can easily be overlooked as a clod of earth. This impression is heightened by the dark brown or grey colouring which can change, although only a little and slowly, to match the surroundings, becoming almost red in a sand pit, for instance. Its jewel-like eyes are golden or coppery-red, and behind them lie the bulges of the parotid glands that contain an acrid, poisonous fluid.

Male toads measure about 2½ in. and the females 1 in. longer.

The common toad ranges over Europe, north and temperate Asia and North Africa. In the British Isles it is widely distributed but is absent from Ireland, the Isle of Man, the Outer Hebrides, Shetland and the Hebridean islands of Tiree and Coll. Unlike the common frog it is found in Orkney.

Toad in the hole

The common toad, like the common frog, hibernates from October to February, but in drier places. Dry banks and disused burrows of small mammals are chosen, and hibernating toads are sometimes found in cellars and outhouses. In the spring they migrate to breeding pools, preferring deeper water than frogs. Where the two are found in the same ponds, the frogs will be in the shallows and the toads in the middle. The migrations of toads are more spectacular. Toads give the impression of being slower movers and the migration route becomes littered with the remains of toads that have fallen foul of enemies. The route is especially well marked where it crosses a road and passing cars have run over the toads.

Although the migration may be long and arduous, perhaps covering 2 or 3 miles at

Heather Angel

639

a rate of ¾ mile in 24 hours, the toads are very persistent, and laboriously climb stone walls and banks.

Outside the breeding season toads live in hollows scooped out by the hindlegs. In soft earth they bury themselves completely, otherwise the hole is made under a log or stone. These homes are usually permanent, the toad returning to the same place day after day. One toad was recorded as living under a front-door step for 36 years until it was attacked by a raven. Occasionally the retreats may be in places that must cost the toad some effort to reach. One is known to have made its home in a privet hedge, 4 ft above the ground, and others have been found in birds' nests.

Every now and then there are stories of toads being found in even odder places. Quarrymen and miners tell of splitting open a rock or lump of coal revealing a cavity in which lies a toad that leaps out hale and hearty. Another story is told of two sawyers working in a saw pit, some 90 years ago. They were sawing the trunk of an oak into planks when they noticed blood dripping out of the wood. Examination revealed the now grisly remains of a toad in a cavity in the trunk. In every story there is speculation as to how the toads came to be imprisoned. It is hardly likely that they were trapped when the coal or rock was first formed millions of years ago, as was once believed. They could not have lived that long, as was shown by the following experiments performed over a century ago. Holes were drilled in blocks of sandstone and limestone, toads put in and the holes sealed with glass plates. The toads in the compact sandstone soon died but the ones in the porous limestone lived for a year or more. These rather macabre experiments suggest that the toads found in rocks and tree trunks could not have been there for long. It is most likely that either they had crawled into a crack or cavity which had later been filled in, or perhaps the miner or quarryman had hit a rock that happened to have a cavity in, thereby causing a toad hidden nearby to leap out suddenly, so creating the impression that it had come out of the hole.

Prey must be moving

At night and during wet weather, toads come out to feed on many kinds of small animals, but they must be moving because toads' eyes are adapted to react to moving objects. Any insect or other small invertebrate is taken, ants being especially favoured, and the stomach of one toad was found to contain 363 ants. Some distasteful animals such as burnet moth caterpillars or caterpillars covered with stiff hairs are left well alone, but toads are known to sit outside beehives in the evening and catch the workers as they come back home. Snails are crunched up and earthworms are pushed into the mouth by the forefeet which also scrape excess earth off them. Young newts, frogs, toads and even slowworms and grass snakes are eaten. One toad had five newly-hatched grass snakes in its stomach, while another had the head of an adder in its mouth. Toads will often return to a favourite retreat after hunting and will use the same home for years.

Spawn in strings

There is little to distinguish the breeding habits of common frogs and common toads. Both breed at roughly the same time of year and may be seen in the same pools. Male toads start arriving before the females but later the males may arrive already in amplexus on the females' backs. There is no external vocal sac and, unlike many of its relatives, a male common toad has a very weak croak.

The spawn is laid in strings rather than in a mass. The eggs are embedded three or four deep in threads of jelly that may be up to 15 ft long. Each female lays 3–4 thousand eggs, which are smaller than those of a frog, being less than 2 mm in diameter.

P Morris

Roy A Harris & KR Duff

The coppery-golden eye of the toad, its most attractive feature, shown with pupil expanded (left) and contracted (right).

Ronan Picture Library

15th-century superstition: extracting the 'faire stone' from the head of a toad.

Strings of spawn rope through the water during mating, to be wrapped around the stems of water plants and convenient pebbles.

The jelly swells up but the spawn does not float, because it is wrapped round the stems of water plants.

The eggs hatch in 10–12 days and the tadpoles develop in the same manner as frog tadpoles, becoming shiny, black, ½in. toadlets in about 3 months. Sexual maturity is reached in 4 years, before the toads are fully grown.

Poisonous toads

Toads suffer from all the enemies to which frogs fall prey, despite the poisonous secretions of the parotid glands. The poison is certainly effective against dogs, that salivate copiously after mouthing a toad, and show all the signs of distress. Sometimes a toad's reaction against grass snakes is to blow up its body as described for burrowing toads.

In old age, toads fall victim to flesh-eating greenbottle flies, which lay their eggs on them. The larvae then crawl into the nostrils, hampering breathing, and eat their way into the toad's body, eventually killing it.

The toad's precious jewel

Toads are often regarded with horror, and in folklore they generally play an unpleasant role. Their mere presence was said to pollute the soil, but one method of preventing this from happening was to plant rue, which toads could not abide. Without it, tragedies could occur of the kind that befell a mediaeval couple strolling in the garden. The young man plucked some leaves of sage, rubbed his teeth with them and promptly fell dead. His young woman was charged with murder and, to prove her innocence, took the judge and court to the garden to demonstrate what had happened, and fell dead too. The judge suspected the cause and had the sage dug up. There was a toad living in the ground beside it.

By contrast, 'the foule Toad has a faire stone in his heade', as the 16th-century writer John Lyly declared. To obtain this jewel the toad was placed on a scarlet cloth which pleased the toad so much that it cast the stone out. The toadstone was then set in a ring, for it had the valuable property of changing colour in the presence of any poison that an enemy might put in food and drink. It was also effective as a cure for snakebite and wasp-stings.

class	**Amphibia**
order	**Salientia**
family	**Bufonidae**
genus & species	***Bufo bufo***

Heather Angel

Conch

The word 'conch' has had a chequered history. Originally applied more to bivalve molluscs it was later taken to include mollusc shells in general, the study of which is still known as conchology. Today it signifies certain large sea-snails whose shells can be converted into trumpets. In a more restricted way it is used as a nickname, applied disparagingly to poorer people, living on the Florida Keys and the Bahamas, who eat the flesh of the large marine snail, Strombus. For this reason Strombus is taken here as typifying the trumpet shells as a whole.

The shells of the members of this genus range in length from ⅝ in. to the 13 in. of S. goliath of Brazil. In some species the lip of the shell is developed in the adult as a heavy projecting wing that stabilizes the shell as it lies on the sea-bed, stopping it from rolling over.

A peculiarity of Strombus is its two large eyes, often ringed with orange, red or yellow, carried on long stalks arising from either side of a stout proboscis. Each stalk has a short tentacle, and the right eye is lodged, when in use, in the 'stromboid notch' in the lip of the shell.

Members of the genus Strombus are world-wide in tropical waters, especially where the temperature does not fall below 70°F. Their distribution is therefore similar to that of coral reefs, and few species are found in waters too cool for reef corals. These conches seem to have originated in the Miocene period in the Tethys Sea, of which the Mediterranean is the largest surviving remnant, and reached their zenith in the Pliocene and Pleistocene periods about 2–11 million years ago. Today there is none in the Mediterranean and there are fewer species elsewhere. The main area is the Indo-Pacific, with 38 species from the Red Sea, Persian Gulf and East Africa eastwards through the Indian Ocean and Malay Archipelago to Hawaii and Easter Island in the Pacific. There are 7 species in the Caribbean, 4 on the Pacific side of Central America, and 1 on the West African coast. Although 2 species live at depths down to 400 ft, most live in shallow water, from low-tide level to 20 ft. They are one of the heavyweight herbivores among shellfish.

The jumping shellfish

Conches move in quite a remarkable way for molluscs. When at rest they tend to bury themselves in sand or gravel but when active they push themselves along with their sharp operculum. The foot of *Strombus* is unlike that of more familiar snails in that only a small part of it is used as a creeping sole in locomotion. The hind end of the foot has an operculum, which in other snails serves as a plate to seal the entrance to the shell when its owner withdraws inside. In *Strombus* it is claw-like with a sharp, often serrated edge, and is used not only in defence, as a sort of dagger against crabs or fish, but to pole the animal along with a kind of leaping action. We cannot better the first account of it, given in 1848 by a Mr Adams who was on board HMS *Samarong* when the ship was in the Caribbean. He wrote in his journal that 'it is, in fact, a most sprightly and energetic animal, and often served to amuse me by its extraordinary leaps and endeavours to escape, planting firmly its powerful narrow operculum against any resisting surface, insinuating it under the edge of its shell, and by a vigorous effort throwing itself forward, carrying its great heavy shell with it, and rolling along in a series of jumps in a most singular and grotesque manner'.

The American zoologist, GH Parker, looked at this more carefully in 1922 and found that Adams was reasonably correct. Parker added a few details, however. He found that each jump carries the conch forward by half the length of its own shell. It pushes the operculum, which is brown and looks like a monstrous overgrown fingernail, into the sand or against a firm object and then presses hard.

Parker pointed out what a remarkable feat this is. For example, the shell of the conch is nearly four times the weight of its soft parts, and the muscles even in this relatively small body are not particularly strong. Granted that the weight of the shell in water is only two-thirds its weight in air, the thrust given by these muscles must still be very powerful. A shell 6 in. long will be carried forward 3 in. and lifted 2 in. off the bottom in the process.

Perhaps more expressive of the power of the thrust is the experience of conch-divers. They dive, gather an armful of conches, then swim to the surface clutching the shellfish tightly to the breast. They often arrive at the surface cut by the sharp edges of the opercula.

Seaweed grazers

The smaller conches graze the deposits of small seaweed fragments that accumulate on the sea-bed. The others crop living seaweeds. The queen conch *Strombus gigas* for example, of Bermuda, Florida, the Caribbean and Brazil, eats the narrow fronds of seaweeds, aligning its vertical

The conch played a large rôle in Aztec culture; the leading priest is blowing a shell-trumpet.

slit-like mouth to them, seizing them with its two ribbed lips. Inside the lips is a pair of jaws as well as the usual rasp-like radula, or horny tongue (see p 6). Fragments of seaweed 1½ in. long have been found in the stomach.

Strings of eggs

During the warmer months conches gather in the shallower water for spawning. The males are usually smaller than the females. After mating the females lay from 200–500 thousand eggs in long jelly-like masses, up to 74 ft long. These strings become coated with sand and coiled and entwined to form spongy masses. In 3–4 days the eggs hatch, releasing free-swimming larvae.

World wide trumpets

The use of large sea-snail shells as trumpets dates from the earliest times and has been widespread across the world, in southern and central Asia, throughout the Indo-Pacific area and in tropical America. In fact, for the archaeologist they have served as a means of tracing the migrations of human communities.

One of the best known today is the conch *Strombus*, but even better known formerly was *Triton*, the shell which figured prominently also in the mythology of Ancient Greece and the preceding civilizations of the eastern Mediterranean. In Greek mythology, the sea-god Triton was Neptune's trumpeter, usually depicted holding a large conch shell, used to call river deities around their monarch. He appears on coins as early as 200 BC, but there is evidence from burials that the conch had a religious or ceremonial significance as early as Neolithic times.

To make a trumpet usually nothing more was done than knock the apex off the shell, but in some instances a hole was made in the top of the shell for a blowhole. A conch has, at various times and places, been used at funerals and weddings, in battle, in churches, at festivals, for raising the alarm, calling for help, driving away devils or invoking the deities, calling home the cattle, summoning labourers and fishermen—indeed, for all purposes for which the brass trumpet or even the modern siren are now used. Even in Mediterranean Europe the conch was still in use until well into the 20th century, and doubtless still persists in some places today.

In Japan, one blast on a triton conch indicated that a riot was under way, two blasts were a fire-alarm, three meant a robbery and four treachery. Of anyone boasting it was said 'Ano hito wa hora wo fuku' (he blows on a conch=blowing his own trumpet).

phylum	**Mollusca**
class	**Gastropoda**
subclass	**Prosobranchia**
order	**Mesogastropoda**
family	**Strombidae**
genus & species	***Strombus goliath*** ***Strombus gigas*** *others*

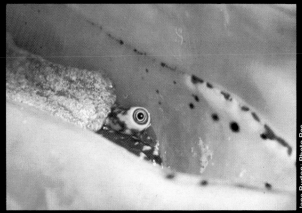

Top: *Stages in the development of the queen conch. Above: A conch, preparing to turn over, digs its foot into the sand.*

The conch is peculiar for its two large eyes, which are carried on two long stalks on both sides of the animal's stout proboscis.

Vulture-like birds, condors have naked heads and necks with vicious hooked beaks.

A 10ft spread and the largest wing area.

Condor

The two largest flying birds in the world, the California condor and the Andean condor, have wingspans of 10 ft. This is less than that of the wandering albatross, but their broad wings give them a much larger wing area, and they weigh 20—25 lb, as much as a good-sized turkey. Yet they would be dwarfed by their extinct relative Teratornis incredibilis of North America that had a wingspan of 16—17 ft.

The condors belong to the same family as the turkey vultures and the other American 'vultures', all of which are unrelated to the true vultures of the Old World except in appearance and habit. The two condors are as ugly as they are large. Both have the repulsive-looking naked head and neck of the true vultures. The California condor has pink skin on the head and its eyes and ears stand out grotesquely behind the powerful hooked bill. Around the neck is a ruff of blackish plumes matching the colour of the body plumage. The Andean condor, which is the slightly larger of the two, is darker around the head and carries a fleshy crest and wrinkles hanging from its face. Around its neck is a neat white ruff.

The rare California condor

At one time the California condor was fairly common and its range extended from northern Oregon to Lower California, eastwards to Nevada and New Mexico, and in prehistoric times it probably spread across the continent. When Europeans started to filter into the western highlands of the United States the California condor could be seen in flocks of 20 or more. Then human settlement destroyed its habitat and reduced the numbers of large mammals whose carcases condors live on, and it was often shot for no particular reason except that it was a large target and that it was thought to spread disease. Others died after eating poisoned carcases put out for wolves. The last wild condor was captured in 1987 to join 26 others in the San Diego Wild Animal Park and the Los Angeles Zoo. The first egg from a captive pair was laid at last in March 1988. Although the Andean condor has already been successfully bred in zoos in South America, the future existence of the Californian condor remains very much in the balance, with no remaining birds left in the wild to replenish stock if the captured condors fail to breed successfully.

The Andean condor is much better off. Although reduced in numbers it is still found over many parts of its range that extends from Venezuela to Patagonia.

A condor may fly over many hundreds of square miles in search of food. This it does almost effortlessly, despite its great weight,

because, like albatrosses, condors are adapted to make the most efficient use of air currents. The condor's method of flight differs from that of the albatross. Instead of gliding up and down in air currents just over the surface, condors, as well as Old World vultures, use rising currents of air to lift them off the ground. These air currents, called thermals, are caused by air heating up near the ground and rising up through the atmosphere. Glider pilots use thermals in the same way as condors. They glide round in a circle within the thermal and the rising air lifts them up. Condors have been recorded at 15 000 ft, gliding over thunderstorms. This is exceptional and condors usually rise no more than a few thousand feet before leaving one thermal and gliding away to another. In this way they are able to quarter their range with hardly a wingbeat.

Carrion eaters

Like the Old World vultures the condors are mainly scavengers. The naked head and neck of both species, like the naked face of the caracaras, seem to be adaptations for carrion-eating. Feathers would become matted with blood from thrusting the head inside the carcases, and a bird cannot preen its own head. On finding a carcase the condors have to wait their turn while the true predators such as golden eagles, wolves and coyotes eat their fill. The remains are then abandoned to the waiting

condors who crowd in, squabbling.

While carrion is their main food condors will also take live lambs, young llamas and deer or wounded animals. Along sea coasts they feed on dead fish and seals and shell-fish, including mussels. Andean condors are known to prey on diving petrels and are sometimes shot because they steal the eggs of guanay cormorants.

A very slow reproductive rate

One reason why condors have suffered especially from persecution is that they breed very slowly. They do not breed until 6 or 7 years, and although they mate for life and may live for 50 years or more, they only lay one egg every other year.

Courtship consists of a dance with the condors walking to and fro hissing and clucking with wings held out. They circle each other, then push and peck until one falls off the ledge where they are nesting. They also chase each other in the air.

The single egg is laid on the bare rock of a ledge or cave in the cliff face. Incubation lasts 7−9 weeks, both sexes participating. The young condor stays with its parents for at least a year and for several years it can be distinguished from adult birds by down covering its head and neck.

A view from a distance

Darwin, Humboldt and other early visitors to South America were very impressed by the majestic flight of the condor and its ability to soar up until lost from sight. But what puzzled zoologists more was their ability to find food, and even more, how when one condor finds a carcase others come flying in to join it. Some authors even write of telepathic communication, but as we learn more about animal behaviour by de-tailed observation the mysteries of their communications are becoming apparent. The orderly weaving and turning of a dense flock of starlings rivals the precision of an acrobatic team and co-ordination of movement is effected by the individuals watching slight movements made by their fellows. For condors it is much simpler; if one condor, soaring high up, sees another suddenly drop to the ground, it knows that it has probably found food, and as this condor glides over to join it its movements are seen by others, who all gather at one spot.

Darwin and others believed that the original discovery of food was made by smelling decomposing matter. Now we know that birds as a whole, condors in-cluded, have a weak sense of smell, and Audubon, the famous ornithologist, showed that condors would land and even attack a model animal, but ignore a carcase covered by a tarpaulin. It seems that sight is the sense used to detect food. The birds of prey (Falconiformes) are noted for ex-tremely sensitive eyesight, and, it must be remembered, their life depends on spotting distant objects, so they must become skilled in detecting a dead animal, or another of their kind, at a distance.

class	**Aves**
order	**Falconiformes**
family	**Cathartidae**
genera & species	***Vultur gryphus*** *Andean condor* ***Gymnogyps californianus*** *California condor*

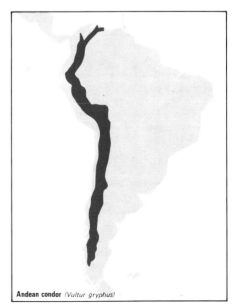

Andean condor *(Vultur gryphus)*

Conus marmoreus

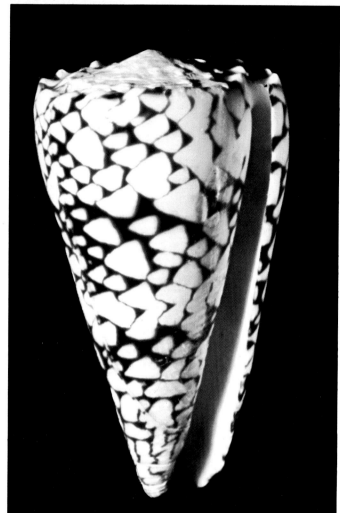

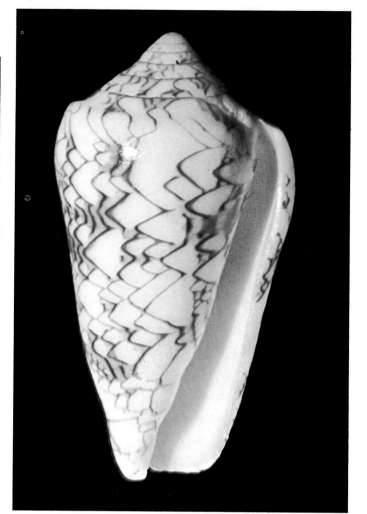

Conus textile

Cone shell

There are 500 to 600 species of cone shells — sea snails named for the shape of their shells. As in an ordinary snail, the shell consists of a tube wrapped round a central column. In the cones the tube is flattened making a long, tapering shell. The cone is formed by the large outside whorl of the tube, with its narrow, slit-like opening extending to the tip of the cone. The base of this cone is formed by the short, and sometimes almost flat, spire formed by the exposed parts of the inner whorls. The surface of the shell is generally smooth with a dotted or lacy pattern of brown on white.

The cones range up to about 9 in. long, the majority being much smaller. Attached to the foot of the mollusc is an elongated operculum, the horny lid or door that seals the aperture of the shell when its owner retires inside. When the snail is active, a pair of sensory tentacles and a long siphon protrude from the front of the body. Water is drawn in through the siphon by the cilia and passed over the gills in the cavity within the shell.

Habits

The cones are found in tropical and sub-tropical waters, mainly in the western Atlantic and around the Philippines and the Malay Archipelago across the Indian Ocean to East Africa, up the Red Sea and in the Mediterranean. They live in shallow water to a depth of several hundred feet. Some live in coral reefs, others in coral sand or rubble. They are active mainly by night, coming out to feed after lying up in crevices or under stones during the day, or burying themselves in the sand with only the siphon showing.

Hunts with a poison harpoon

The cones are carnivorous, feeding on worms, other molluscs or even live fish such as blennies or gobies, each species having its own preferred prey, which it first paralyses and then swallows whole. Capture of the prey is accomplished by means of a snout-like proboscis armed with long poisonous teeth. The teeth are basically the same structures as those on the tongue or radula of other snails, such as the abalone (see p. 11) or banded snail. In most snails there are many small teeth forming a file for scraping off particles of food, but in the cones there are only a few teeth, each as much as $\frac{3}{8}$ in. long. Each tooth is a long, barbed, hollow

harpoon mounted on a mobile stalk. Associated with these teeth is a poison gland, connected by a long tube to the teeth. The viscous, milky white poison is squeezed out by the contraction of muscles around the poison gland.

Cone shells detect scent particles secreted by their prey with a sense organ called the osphradium, which 'tastes' the water as it is drawn through the siphon. A fish-eating cone shell will respond if water from a tank containing fish is put in its own tank.

The cone will either track down its prey, if it is another slow-moving animal such as a worm or mollusc, or lie in wait. The final stages of attack are controlled by touch. The proboscis is brought out of its sheath and held poised, then brought rapidly down onto the prey. At the same time a single tooth is everted and thrust into the victim's body. In seconds it is paralysed by the poison and the cone shell can eat it at leisure. The mouth at the end of the proboscis dilates and engulfs the victim's body, rapid muscular contractions forcing it down the gullet with the help of a lubricating secretion. Swallowing and digestion may take several hours, and during this time the snail cannot retreat into the shell.

The tooth usually breaks off when it has been used and another is brought forward

Conus striatus (worn)

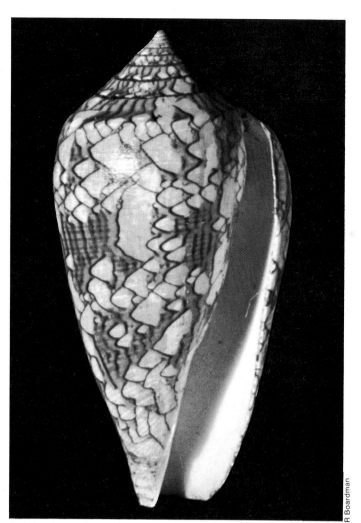

Conus textile

for the next victim. The poison is related to curare (the famous arrow poison of American Indians) and paralyses the victim's muscles. If the prey is another mollusc the paralysis makes it lose its grip on its shell so the cone can draw it out.

Breeding

The eggs are laid in vase-shaped capsules of a hard, parchment-like material. The capsules are attached by their bases in lines or groups to the coral or rock. They hatch in about 10 days.

The Glory of the Sea

Their beauty has resulted in cones being used for money, in the manner of cowries, and Rembrandt was sufficiently impressed by the marbled cone *Conus marmoreus* to depict it in his etching of 1650, 'The Little Horn'. Careful as ever to etch his signature in mirror image, he neglected to do the same for the shell which therefore twists the wrong way in the print.

The shells are also highly esteemed by collectors and of all shells the one that has been held most precious is the rare Glory of the Sea, *Conus gloriamaris*. Its shell has a fine network pattern of pink-brown on a light background. Although a most beautiful shell, it was its rarity that once tempted an American collector to pay $2 000 for a specimen, and others regularly change hands for several hundred dollars. The earliest record of the Glory of the Sea is in a catalogue of 1757 when a specimen was sold at the Zoological Museum of Copenhagen. A few other specimens were found later, but towards the end of the 19th century the species was considered by some people to have become extinct as a result of the destruction of the reef which was its only known home. In fact, specimens had been found elsewhere before this, but many years passed before the next came to light in 1957, when one was found in the Philippines. Since then a number of others have been found off Indonesia, the Philippines and in the sea east of New Guinea, so that by 1966 over 50 had been found and the Glory of the Sea was no longer the most prized of shells.

The poisonous teeth with which the cones despatch their prey present a great danger to the collector who must pick up the living animals with extreme caution. Some, like the Mediterranean species *C. mediterraneus* are too puny to be troublesome and others may sting no more severely than a bee, but in other cases the pain may be excruciating and even fatal, death ensuing in 4 or 5 hours. One survey gives the death rate as 20% of all people stung, higher than that due to cobra or rattlesnake. When the cone stings it does so very rapidly and the victim may at first be unaware of the attack. Pain comes later, together with numbness, blurred vision and difficulty in breathing. A Japanese collector who was stung by the geographer cone *C. geographus* was able to walk just over a mile before collapsing, and dying of heart and breathing failure. The Glory of the Sea and many others are also very poisonous, and with the increase in the number of people collecting shells with aqua-lung apparatus, the number of deaths is sure to rise.

phylum	**Mollusca**	
class	**Gastropoda**	
sub-class	**Prosobranchia**	
order	**Stenoglossa**	
super-family	**Toxoglossa**	*arrow tongues*
family	**Conidae**	
genus	***Conus***	

Conger

The conger is a stout-bodied marine eel, normally up to 4—5 ft long but may reach 9 ft or more and a weight of 100 lb. There is an unconfirmed weight for 1940 of 160 lb. The body is scaleless, brown to dark slate and the underside may be silvery. The colour varies according to the sea-bed; on a sandy bottom being more or less colourless, and dark on a gravel bottom or among rocks. The gill-openings are large and extend to the underside of the body. The mouth runs backwards to below the level of the eye and is armed with rows of sharp teeth, one row in the upper jaw being set so close together they form a cutting edge. The front pair of nostrils are tubular, each of the hind pair being opposite the centre of the front edge of the eye. The eyes are large, reminiscent of those of deep-sea fishes. The pectoral fins are fairly large, the pelvics are lacking. The dorsal fin begins from above the pectorals, is continuous along the back and runs into the anal fin.

Congers are often called conger-eels. This is unnecessary. The name is from the Latin congrus *meaning sea-eel.*

The conger lives off rocky coasts, in the north and south Atlantic, Mediterranean, Indian and Pacific Oceans, but is not found on the west coast of the Americas. It also lives in deeper water, down to 660 ft or more.

Graceful acrobat

The conger swims easily and gracefully. When cruising it is propelled largely by wave-like movements passing down the dorsal and anal fins, from the front backwards. At greater speeds the body moves in a serpentine, side-to-side undulation. Not uncommonly it turns on its side to swim by undulating movements of the body. When doing this at the surface it presents a series of humps rather like those of the legendary sea-serpent. It spends the day lying among rocks or in crevices, sometimes on its back, periodically yawning, an action probably connected with respiration rather than fatigue. Congers are given to somewhat lethargic 'acrobatics', remaining poised head-down, sometimes doing so at the surface with a third or more of the body sticking up vertically out of the water. Or they may contort the body into other odd postures, holding each position for a perceptible time.

No flesh refused

Congers are carnivorous, taking any animal food including carrion and even smaller congers. Crabs and lobsters are held in the mouth and battered against rocks before being swallowed. The voracity of congers can be judged by stories of men having fingers bitten off when sorting a catch in which a conger lies hidden, or having a finger seized when feeling in rock crevices and having to cut it off to avoid being held

DP Wilson

Congers are distinguished from freshwater eels by their complete lack of scales. Their powerful jaws have a formidable battery of teeth—and a vice-like grip. With jaws agape, they often lurk in rocky crevices waiting to slip out after their prey.

and drowned when the tide came in. There is a story of a conger biting off the heel of a fisherman's sea-boot.

Thin-headed larvae

Like the freshwater eel the conger spawns once and then dies. The congers of European Atlantic waters spawn near the Sargasso Sea at depths of 10 200 ft in late summer. There is another spawning ground in the Mediterranean. Before spawning congers stop feeding, become almost black with very much enlarged eyes, especially in the male, and then look like deep-sea fishes. The female lays 3—8 million eggs, each $\frac{1}{10}$ in. diameter. These float in the intermediate layers of the ocean but occasionally reach the surface.

The first eel larva, of the freshwater eel, was found in 1777 and named *Leptocephalus* (thin-head) by the Italian naturalist Scopoli, under the impression that it was a new kind of fish. The first conger larva was found in 1763 by William Morris, of Holyhead, but was not described until 1788, when the German scientist Johann Gmelin named it *Leptocephalus morrisii*. And it was not until 1864 that it was recognized to be the larval stage of the conger. Even then, Albert Gunther, distinguished ichthyologist, held that it was a kind of freak, a case of arrested development. In 1886, however, Yves Delage the French zoologist proved beyond doubt that *Leptocephalus morrisii* was a larval conger by watching a leptocephalus change into a young conger in an aquarium. Later in the 19th century the true nature of what are now called the leptocephali became more firmly established when the Italian naturalist Raffaele managed to keep eggs and larvae of five species of eel alive in aquaria.

The conger leptocephali lose their larval teeth, on reaching coastal waters after their journey across the Atlantic, and change into young eels. The body becomes rounded and

eel-like and its length drops from 5 to 3 in. Until they reach a length of 15 in. the young congers are a pale pink. After this they gradually take on the dark colour of the adult. When about 2 ft long they move down the continental shelf, and beyond, into water more than 600 ft deep, and spend most of their time on the bottom.

Tons of floating conger

Dr Frank Buckland, in his *Curiosities of Natural History,* has recorded the observations made during January and February, 1855, by a surgeon who lived at St Leonards on the southeast coast of England: 'During the intense cold, some few miles out at sea, *thousands* of conger-eels were found floating on the surface of the water. They could progress readily in any direction, but could not descend, and consequently fell an easy prey, the boatmen catching them by means of hooks on the end of a long stick. In this manner no less than *eighty tons* were captured, of all sizes, some being as much as six feet long, and of a surprising circumference. The greater part of them were sent to London per rail. One of them I opened, and found the air-vessel (that is, swimbladder) distended with air to the utmost, so as to completely close the valvular opening. It was this, evidently, that buoyed them up.'

class	**Osteichthyes**
order	**Anguilliformes**
family	**Congridae**
genus & species	*Conger conger*

648

Conservation

An African elephant that has fallen victim to poachers. A snare was used to trap the elephant, which was then killed by poisoned arrow. A white trickle of poison can be seen oozing from the wound. However, on this occasion the poachers were disturbed before they could remove the ivory tusks.

Norman Myers: Bruce Coleman Ltd.

Conservation, ecology and environment are words in common use, and hardly a day passes without their appearing in the newspapers or being mentioned on radio or television. Nearly everyone has some idea of the meaning of these words, but the interpretations can vary widely. Most governments now express some degree of concern about the environment, and a great deal of legislation of one sort or another has been enacted in recent years. We are constantly reminded by politicians of the need to conserve the world's non-renewable natural resources; we are asked by conservation organizations to make financial contributions to help save the rhinos of Africa and Asia, or the whales of the oceans; we may be asked by a local action group to sign a petition to protest

against the draining of a piece of marshland, to stop a wood being felled, or some open country from being built over. The past decade or so has seen a whole succession of international conferences on a wide range of conservation and environmental matters. Thousands of articles on these subjects have been published in magazines, hundreds of books have appeared in print, and large numbers of films dealing with wildlife and environmental matters have been screened to television. Last but not least, we have been warned of all kinds of impending ecological crises. It is truly the age of environmental awareness. Even large industrial companies have recognized the situation by employing ecologists, by subsidizing the making of wildlife films, by sponsoring books

on natural history, and by giving grants towards the purchase of nature reserves, just to mention some of the ways in which big business has reacted to public opinion. Just about everybody seems to be jumping on the conservation bandwagon, and there are a bewildering variety of organizations involved. But just what is conservation and ecology all about?

Definitions

Ecology is relatively easy to define, and basically it means the study of living organisms, including man, in relation to their environment, and it is a rapidly developing science. The conservation of wildlife and wildlife habitats often requires the application of ecological knowledge. It is quite difficult to say exactly when conservation, in the sense in which it is understood today, had its beginnings for it is a concept that has evolved over a considerable period of time.

The need for conservation

Conservation, ecology and the environment are all inter-linked and cannot be considered in isolation. There is plenty of evidence that many primitive peoples practised a form of conservation in that they did not over-exploit the wildlife resources upon which they depended for food and clothing. The African natives hunting the abundant game of the savanna and the Red Indians hunting the buffalo on the vast North American prairies lived in good harmony with their environment. The problems began when the world's population started to increase by leaps and bounds, and man's technology became ever more advanced. The invention of the firearm, for example, had a profound effect on wildlife as it made indiscriminate slaughter easy; the North American buffalo was brought to the verge of extinction as a result of shooting by the white man. Man has, of course, been modifying his environment in one way or another for thousands of years, by clearing ground for agriculture, cutting trees for fuel and so on. The difference now is easily summarized – an ever increasing human population is rapidly depleting the world's renewable and non-renewable resources, including wildlife. In addition, man is creating massive ecological upheaval and stress by polluting the seas and the atmosphere with a variety of toxic substances, by changing the nature of vast areas of land and even local climates, and by means of massive development projects and the large-scale destruction of forests and other natural habitats.

There are many examples around the world of man's technological achievements New Zealand, for example, has some of the largest man-made forests of alien conifers in the world; in Rhodesia in 1955 construction began of the huge Kariba Dam across the Zambesi River which, when completed, created the largest man-made lake in the world; the James Bay hydroelectric scheme in Canada will, when completed in a few years time, affect an area of about 214 050 square miles. Many other examples could be quoted, and there is no shortage of ideas for other equally large-scale projects. The Russians, for instance, have talked of a plan to dam the Bering Straits. Despite man's apparent ability to do much as he likes with the environment, most intelligent people now realize that man is not above the laws of nature. He is just another animal, albeit a highly intelligent one, and part of the world's ecosystems. His survival depends, as does that of other animals, on the health and quality of the planet earth. This realization is perhaps one of the most significant changes in outlook in recent years.

Animal sanctuaries

Conservation is now largely based on ecological research, but the early initial approach to the subject was for the most part uncritical and emotive. Thinking tended to be in terms of saving beautiful animals or attractive wild scenery. The answer to the first was the establishment of sanctuaries for particular

Lake Nakuru in Kenya, one of the many national parks of Africa, is famous for its flamingoes.

Eric Hosking

species, and these at first seemed satisfactory, but in those early days there was little understanding of animal population dynamics or habitat conservation. We now know that inviolable sanctuaries are rarely the way to ensure the perpetuation of a species or a natural community, and the management of a nature reserve requires the skilled application of scientific techniques.

The national parks of many countries are now an important aspect of wildlife and habitat conservation, but the early examples were mainly seen as a means of protecting beautiful or wild scenery. There is no doubt at all about who invented the national park concept, it was the United States who established the world's first national park at Yellowstone, Wyoming, in 1872. The idea caught on fast; Canada established the Rocky Mountain (now Banff) National Park in 1885, Australia the Royal National Park in Sydney in the same year, New Zealand the Tongariro National Park in 1894, and in South Africa the Sabie Game Reserve, designated in 1898, became the Kruger National Park in 1926. There are now a considerable number of national parks that are of major importance for wildlife, as for example those in East and South Africa, where the Kruger National Park is the third largest and one of the richest in wildlife in the world. In Kenya there are about a dozen animal reserves of one sort or another, such as Aberdare, Lake Nakuru and Mount Kenya National Parks, and the Amboseli, Masai and Meru Game Reserves. In the national parks complete protection of the fauna and flora is the primary purpose, and human utilization of the land is in theory precluded. In the game reserves conservation of wildlife is still the primary objective, but some native activities such as grazing are sometimes allowed. In most African countries from 5½ to 15% of

the land is now permanently protected by national parks or other statutory designations. The importance of national parks cannot be over-emphasized, particularly where they include habitat types that are under threat, as for example tropical rain forest. In 1979 the Central American countries of Costa Rica and Panama announced their intention of designating a national park of about 250 000 acres of mountains and forests straddling the borders of the two countries, and Panama also established the 60 000 acre Parque Naçional de la Libertad which includes important virgin rain forest with its associated fauna.

Conservation in Britain

The study of natural history, from which the conservation philosophy in Europe gradually evolved, can probably be justifiably claimed as a British initiative, and the network of local natural history societies (many of them with more than 100 years of tradition behind them) still survives. Among the famous names of the earlier years that come to mind are those of Thomas Pennant and Gilbert White. Then there was Charles Darwin whose classic work *The Origin of Species* revolutionized biological thinking. Much of the earlier interest in natural history revolved, as it still does to a very great extent, around birds. One of the first bird protection acts in Britain was passed in 1869 to protect seabirds on the Yorkshire cliffs. Further legislation in 1870, 1873, 1877 and 1880 gave protection to the great crested grebe *Podiceps cristatus*, whose breeding population in Britain had sunk to about 32 pairs by 1860 as a result of persecution. An important event in Britain in 1889 was the formation of the Royal Society for the Protection of Birds (RSPB). By the summer of 1989 the membership of the RSPB was in excess of

In the 1850s the population of greater crested grebes fell to below 40 pairs due to the use of their feathers in hat-making.

540,000; the society manages 114 reserves totalling over 100,000 acres. Its influence in the field of conservation extends well beyond the shores of Britain. In the United States the Sierra Club came into being in 1892 and the National Audubon Society at the turn of the century. Both of these organizations are dedicated to the conservation and appreciation of wiidlife and wilderness, and to maintaining the integrity of ecosystems. The Sierra Club operates not only in the USA but in other countries also.

It may well be that conservation in the sense in which it is understood today was first conceived by Nathaniel Charles Rothschild (1877–1923) who, years ahead of his time, realized the importance of protecting and conserving habitats rather than the

individual species threatened with extinction, and of the necessity of massive publicity and government support. He founded the Society for the Promotion of Nature Reserves in 1912. This is now the Royal Society for Nature Conservation with 184,000 member and is the coordinating body for the voluntary naturalists' trusts movement in Britain. The first of these trusts came into being in Norfolk in 1929 and there are now 48 trusts in England and Wales, plus another in Ulster and the Scottish Wildlife Trust. The trusts in England and Wales now manage a total of 1036 reserves with a combined area of 58,407 acres, and the Scottish Wildlife Trust has 47 reserves which total 21,670. The combined membership of these trusts is more than 204,000.

An anti-poaching patrol in the Royal Chitwan National Park, Nepal.

Charles Rothschild was a man of vision who saw Britain as part of the overall European conservation scene, and in November 1913 he addressed a conference on the international protection of nature, held at Berne in Switzerland, and in 1914 he was elected United Kingdom representative to the Consultative Committee for the International Protection of Nature. But even before this, he had already begun to collect data for Australia and New Zealand, and subsequently developed ideas regarding conservation in India, the Seychelles, and a number of British Crown Colonies. For various reasons most of the concepts that he had formulated lapsed until 1948 when the International Union for the Protection of Nature was formed. This is now the International Union for the Conservation of Nature and Natural Resources (IUCN) based in Switzerland, and a very potent force on the world conservation scene.

Two important events took place in Britain in 1949. In that year the National Parks and Access to the Countryside Act was passed, and the Nature Conservancy was established by the government. This became the Nature Conservancy Council (NCC) in 1973. The advice of the skilled staff of the NCC has been sought by many countries around the world in the course of developing their conservation policies, but the organization's main function concerns nature conservation in Britain. It has now established some 165 National Nature Reserves covering 325 803 acres. Under the National Parks and Access to the Countryside Act of 1949, local authorities, with the agreement of the NCC, can declare statutory Local Nature Reserves, and there are now 69 of these in the British Isles. On a wider front, 1949 also saw the holding of the first International Technical Conference on the Protection of Nature, held

651

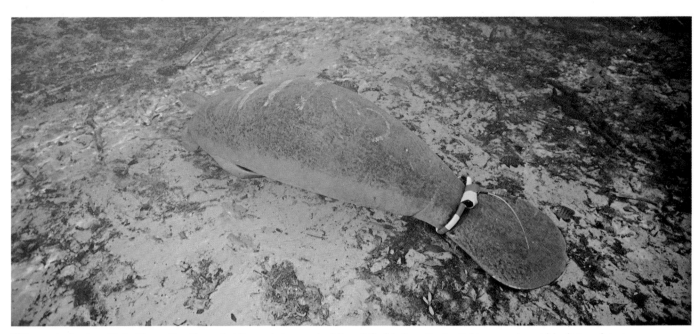

M. Timothy O'Keefe: Bruce Coleman Ltd.

This manatee has been fitted with a radio collar so that its wanderings can be followed. Such information is vital in conserving widely-dispersed species.

in New York and organized by IUCN and the United Nations Educational, Scientific and Cultural Organisation (UNESCO).

International conservation

This necessarily selective review has brought the story to the late 1940's and in the following years there were numerous developments in the field of international conservation. The 1950's and 1960's saw the dawning of what is now universally known as the Environmental Revolution. It marked the point where the long struggle of a small minority to secure the conservation of nature was overtaken by a great tide of awakening mass public opinion reacting against degradation of the environment. This reaction was fuelled by such events as the publication of Rachel Carson's famous book *Silent Spring* in 1962, and the wreck of the supertanker *Torrey Canyon* off the British coast in 1967. So much has happened in the last 25–30 years that only a selection of the more important developments can be mentioned. In 1961 the World Wildlife Fund (WWF) was formed. This organization works on an international basis, primarily through the medium of national appeals whose main functions are to educate the public and raise money for conservation. There are now national appeals in 26 countries, and up to July 1979 the WWF had financed 2188 projects at a cost of some £20 million. The headquarters of the WWF are in Switzerland in the same building as the IUCN with which they work very closely. There can be little doubt that IUCN and the WWF are the most important non-governmental organizations on the world conservation scene, and they work closely with official international organizations such as UNESCO, the United Nations Environment Programme (UNEP) and the Food and Agriculture Organization (FAO). A typical example of a joint IUCN/WWF project was the Seas Must Live Campaign launched in 1977/1978, and directed towards a global marine conservation strategy.

A very successful American initiative was the First World Conference on National Parks, held in Seattle in 1962. Attended by representatives of 63 countries this splendid conference managed at one stroke to bring into existence a close-knit international group of national park managers and promoters, and to give a powerful impetus to the national parks movement worldwide. It is encouraging that so many of the developing countries have embraced the national parks concept with enthusiasm. As mentioned earlier, nature conservation cannot be divorced from environmental problems in general, and equally environmental problems cannot be dealt with in isolation from economics and politics. International action and cooperation is essential, and a milestone in this respect was the United Nations Conference on the Human Environment, held in Stockholm in 1972.

Conservation in action

Endangered species of fauna and flora are very much a matter of international concern, and the production of a series of constantly revised *Red Data Books* by IUCN has served to define and quantify the problem. The Convention on International Trade in Endangered Species of Wild Fauna and Flora (CITES) was signed in Washington in 1973, and is now adhered to by 80 countries. CITES is designed to control the lucrative international trade in such things as living rare birds and animals, ivory, turtle shells, and the furs and skins of rare species.

The launching of campaigns by conservation organizations is an important part of their operations. In New Zealand in the early 1970s the Native Forests Action Coun-

Oil pollution is becoming an increasing problem. Birds that become covered in oil have little chance of survival and whole colonies of breeding birds can be wiped out.

Eric Hosking

cil initiated a nationwide campaign to gain public support for their fight against the proposals of the New Zealand Forest Service to log much of the remaining native evergreen forest. Later, the Royal Forest and Bird Society launched a similar campaign relative to the effects of selective logging on the kokako *Callaeas cinerea*, one of New Zealand's endangered birds. Many types of habitat around the world are threatened in various ways. One example are wetlands, thousands of acres of which have been lost because of drainage, reclamation for agriculture, or simply from pollution. The European Information Centre for Nature Conservation launched a European Wetlands Campaign in 1976/1977. Similarly, in 1979, the RSPB in Britain announced its Silver Meadows Campaign to raise money for the purchase of low lying grassland flood meadows, which are now one of Britain's threatened habitats. Other campaigns are concerned with particular species, and the WWF declared 1979 the Year of the Rhino, with the aim of coordinating efforts to ensure the future of the five species of rhino in Africa and Asia.

It is likely that many of the conservation issues of the future will be dealt with internationally, frequently at government level, and will be the subject of legislation based on sound ecological data. In December 1978, for example, the European Economic Community (EEC) agreed a Directive on Bird Conservation which lays down minimum standards of protection to which all member countries will have to conform. Also, in 1978, IUCN issued the first draft of its *World Conservation Strategy*, the final version of which was unveiled in London in March 1980. Such developments do not mean that there is no place for non-governmental organizations or concerned individuals. Their role will be of great importance in such matters as public education, the collection of essential data,

pressurizing of politicians, and fund-raising. Activity at the local level is just as important as the high-powered activities of international lawyers and politicians. It is the enthusiasts at the grass roots of the movement who do much of the actual physical work of conservation.

It has to be recognized that very little in nature stands still, and wildlife and habitat conservation is dealing with a dynamic situation. Also, it is essential that many of the problems be viewed in their global context. Both habitats and animal populations will, for the most, part, need to be scientifically managed, although in some cases the amount of management required may be minimal. Whilst rare species may need every encouragement to increase their numbers, other species may be so abundant in certain areas that their numbers will require culling in order that they do not destroy their own habitat, as happened with the elephants of Kenya's Tsavo National Park in the early 1960's.

Around the city of Ottawa in the Province of Ontario, Canada, there is a large population of the North American beaver *Castor canadensis*. For the most part the animals and the human population live in harmony, and this is so because there is an active policy of beaver management. Nuisance animals may be live-trapped and released elsewhere where there are few beavers, and in winter controlled kill-trapping is carried out in order to keep the numbers in any given area to the level that the habitat can support. This is just one example of wildlife management that benefits both parties.

The future of conservation

There is a subtle difference in the attitude to wildlife between the northern (developed) countries and the southern (developing or Third World) countries. In the north wildlife is seen as part of man's cultural and ethical

A North American beaver and its dam. Sensible conservation measures and habitat management have ensured the survival of this animal.

heritage and is protected as such. For those developing countries which still have abundant wildlife (and some do not), it is likely to be regarded as a rich natural resource, and as a potential source of wealth for their peoples. Provided that this resource is utilized on a sustainable yield basis, this attitude must be accepted. The long-term survival of national parks, virgin forests and wildlife in the Third World may well depend on the contribution they can make to the welfare of the human populations of those countries. The newly independent state of Papua New Guinea, for example, has made significant advances towards the sustainable management of a number of wildlife resources, including birds of paradise, butterflies, crocodiles and seashells. Both butterflies and crocodiles, for instance, are 'farmed', which takes the pressure off wild populations.

Conservation in the future, if it is to be successful, will require the support and participation of everyone, from the man in the street who feeds birds in the garden, right up the ladder to national governments. The tools for the job will be legislation; education; ecological research; the manipulation of existing habitats, and sometimes the creation of new ones; active management of wildlife populations, often on a sustainable yield basis; the implementation of scientifically based programmes to restore degraded habitats, and to aid the recovery of endangered species, sometimes by breeding them in captivity for subsequent release into the wild.

The achievements in the field of conservation over the past 10–15 years in particular have been considerable. Yet set against the depletion, degradation and outright destruction of ecosystems and species, many of the achievements seem small, fragmented and possibly ephemeral. There must be even better achievements in the future, which is exactly what IUCN's World Conservation Strategy, the first ever analysis of global conservation problems, is all about.

Conservation has triumphed in the case of the Hawaiian goose, or ne-ne. Having been nearly extinct in 1950 it has since been successfully re-established in the wild from stock bred at Slimbridge in England.

Return to the nest. Coots prefer to nest among beds of reeds and water plants.

HM Barnfather : Photo Res

Coot

Coots swim well in the water because they have developed on each toe lobed flaps which act as paddles; these leave the toes free, unlike the webbed feet of ducks, so the bird is also very nimble on land.

Coots also have a white shield on the forehead, an extension of the bill. In the horned coot of South America, the shield is replaced by wattles and a fleshy horn or caruncle. The 10 kinds of coot are members of the rail family which includes the corncrake and moorhen and is related to the cranes.

The main home of coots is in South America, where seven kinds are found, including the horned coot and the giant coot that live in lonely lakes high in the Andes. The other three coots are very similar. The American coot, with a grey plumage, is found from central Canada to Ecuador and Colombia, the common or European coot extends from the British Isles to Japan, and the barely distinguishable

crested or knob-billed coot ranges from southern Spain, throughout Africa to Cape Town.

An aggressive diver

Outside the breeding season coots gather in flocks of hundreds or thousands. They are found on fairly large bodies of water, compared with the related moorhen which can be seen on small ponds and streams.

During the breeding season coots keep to beds of reeds and other water plants where they can be seen threading their way through the stems, the white frontal shield drawing attention to the slow nodding of the head that accompanies the paddling. Sometimes they come out of the cover and can be seen leisurely crossing the pond in a straight line, headed for another clump of reeds. When alarmed, they run across the water with wings beating, leaving a trail of splashes, to subside with a crash and disappear into cover. At other times they will dive, neatly upending and disappearing below the surface leaving scarcely a ripple. They are on record as staying under for 27 seconds and descending to 24 ft.

Coots are not noted for the power of their

flight, being rarely seen in the air. Take-off is long and laborious as they taxi over the water, but once airborne coots are capable of sustained flight and they are known to migrate regularly between the British Isles and the Continent.

Aggressive quarrelling is a feature of the coots' life that has often been remarked on. Both in the winter flocks and during the breeding season when pairs defend their territories, coots can be seen fighting, sending up sheets of water but rarely coming to blows. The first sign of aggression is the adoption of an aggressive posture by one or both coots, with head down and wings arched. If one does not retreat they swim together then suddenly erupt into a water-throwing match like bathers at the seaside. They sit back on their tails and splash water over each other by beating with the wings and feet. The contest is usually over in a few seconds, after which one may retreat, hotly pursued by the other.

Weed-eaters

Coots eat mainly water plants, diving down and bringing up masses of weed which is eaten on the surface. They also come on land to eat grass and even acorns. This diet is supplemented by animal food, including small fish, tadpoles, water insects, molluscs and worms. Occasionally they raid the nests of black-headed gulls and grebes, piercing the eggs and sipping the contents, and sometimes ducklings have been killed.

Floating island nests

Typically, coots make their nests among the tall water plants around the margins of lakes, building up a mass of dead reeds, flags and other leaves often rising 1 ft above water level and having a slipway for easier access. If the water level rises more vegetation is added to keep the eggs dry. Other nests, such as those made by the giant coot, are floating platforms of vegetation sometimes anchored to the stems of living water plants, but the nearby horned coots build their nests on natural hummocks or even make their own. On one lake horned coots were found to be making their nests of vegetation on piles of stones up to 6 ft high and 13 ft in diameter. The piles never broke the surface of the lake but had 1−2 ft of vegetation on top. Further observation showed that the nests were actually made by the horned coots. Pebbles were collected from the lake shore or the lake bed and carried in the bill to the pile, but as stones 11 lb. in weight were found in the pile this cannot have been the only method of transport, but, as yet, no one has seen how the coots manage such heavy weights. As it is, the building of the pile must be a very arduous business, although it is used from year to year with more stones being added each season.

Coots lay from March onwards in the British Isles. Usually 6−9 eggs are laid, but there may be as many as 15. Both parents incubate and the eggs hatch in just over 3 weeks. At first the female broods them while the male brings food, but after a few days the chicks leave the nest, returning at night to be brooded.

At first the parents do not specifically recognise their own chicks but will accept

Coot chicks are fed by the parents for one month, when they begin to fend for themselves

▽ *Coots have developed feet with lobed flaps on each toe, which make very efficient paddles.*

old the chicks begin diving for their own food and the down changes to a uniform blackish colour, relieved by dirty-white throat and underparts.

There are two, or sometimes three, broods a year and the older chicks help their parents to raise the nest in times of flood and will bring food for the younger chicks.

Coots' aerial defence

Now that birds of prey are rare coots do not have many enemies but sea-eagles, hawks, especially harriers, and greater black-backed gulls prey on them. Outside the breeding season, when the coots are living on large stretches of open water, their defence is based on safety in numbers. They keep close together in large rafts that make it difficult for an enemy to single out any individual for attack. As the raft moves slowly forward, some coots get left behind feeding, but they soon rush to catch up the raft when the gap between them widens. Bunching together is a common method of defeating aerial enemies. Black-headed gulls, for example, fly around in tight formation when peregrines are sighted. Coots do much the same but on water.

Sometimes the coots' defence is more active. They have been seen to throw up a shower of spray in the face of a hawk as it swoops down on the flock. Considering the amount of spray sent up by a pair of coots when fighting, a flock must put up quite an effective barrage.

and feed any chick about the same size as their own. Chicks considerably larger or smaller are, however, attacked and even killed if they do not retreat. Later, when their own chicks are about a fortnight old, the parents recognise them as individuals and no other chick is allowed in the territory. At the same time the chicks, which used to beg food from any adult, now solicit only from their parents.

The young chicks are clad in a sooty down but their heads are brilliantly coloured. Around the bill, which is white with a black tip and shading to vermilion on the frontal shield, is a patch of red down. The sides of the face are orange, the crown blue and the nape red, orange or black. When a month

class	**Aves**
order	**Gruiformes**
family	**Rallidae**
genus & species	***Fulica americana*** *American coot* **F. atra** *European coot* **F. cornuta** *horned coot* **F. cristata** *crested or knob-billed coot* **F. gigantea** *giant coot*

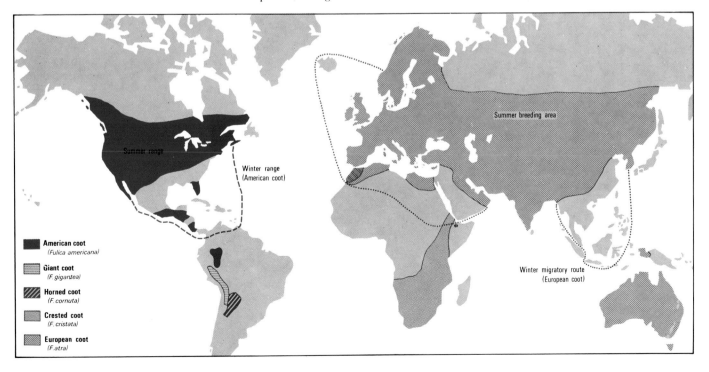

American coot
(Fulica americana)

Giant coot
(F. gigantea)

Horned coot
(F. cornuta)

Crested coot
(F. cristata)

European coot
(F. atra)

Summer range

Winter range
(American coot)

Summer breeding area

Winter migratory route
(European coot)

Copper butterfly

The wings of these butterflies have the colour and lustre of polished copper and are marked with dark spots and bands, sometimes with blue or purple as well. They are a group of small butterflies in the family Lycaenidae, and are thus allied to the blues and hairstreaks. They are widely distributed in the temperate and cold regions of the northern hemisphere, both in the Old and the New World. There are, however, three species in temperate New Zealand. Presumably their ancestors arose from the same stock as those in the northern hemisphere and in time became separated.

The caterpillars are slug-shaped and, in the majority of species, feed on various kinds of dock or sorrel. Like those of many of the blues (see p. 382) the larvae of some species are attended by ants for the sake of a sweet secretion which they produce. In the case of the coppers this exudes all over the body, unlike many others of the family, which have a single orifice connected with a special gland.

Two species are associated with Britain, one as a familiar butterfly of fields, downland and open country in general, the other as an insect which unhappily became extinct quite recently. They are known respectively as the small copper and the large copper.

Small copper

This is a pretty, lively and even rather aggressive little butterfly. The males establish territories and try to chase all other butterflies away, flying out and attacking individuals of their own species and other, larger ones as well. They have no weapons and are quite incapable of injuring each other.

The small copper is found all over the British Isles and has an enormous range extending from Europe right across Asia to Japan, over a large part of North America and northward to beyond the Arctic Circle. It is divided into distinct subspecies in different parts of its range but they are all very similar in appearance. Some of these subspecies range into Africa. Another ranges almost as far north as any butterfly, into Ellesmere Land, and is one of the five butterflies found in Greenland.

Three generations a year

The larva feeds on dock and sorrel and the life cycle is passed through so quickly that there may be three generations in a good summer. The caterpillar is green with a brown line along the back and clothed with short greyish hairs. It is not attended by ants. The pupa is pale brown or greenish and attached to a leaf or stem of the food plant. The species overwinters as a larva but not (as in most larval hibernators) at any particular stage of its growth. The butterfly is on the wing continuously from May to October.

The small copper is exceedingly variable, and its more extreme varieties or 'aberrations' are eagerly sought by collectors. Re-

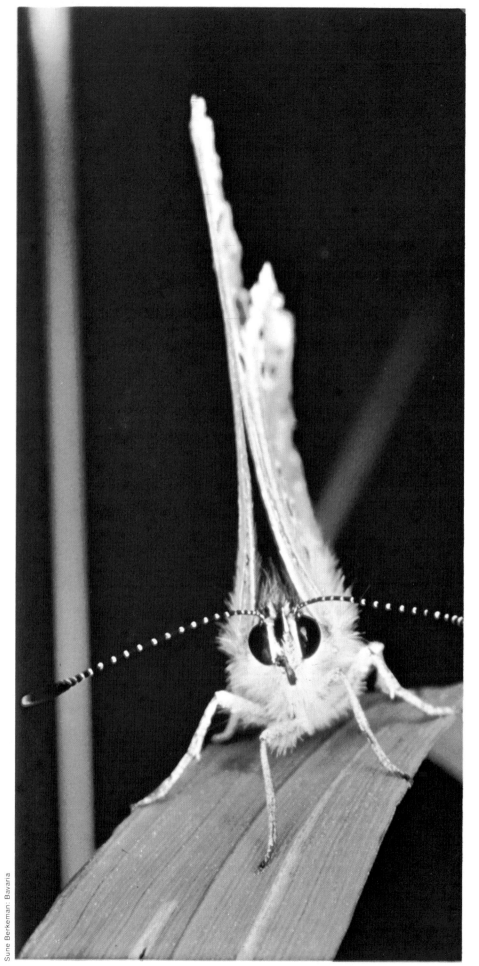

Sune Berkeman: Bavaria

◁ *Small copper at rest. These far-ranging butterflies often breed three times a year.*

△ *A small copper shows its wing pattern while taking a meal off a sprig of heather.*

▽ *One of the Dutch large coppers introduced to Wood Walton Fen on great water dock plant.*

duction or modification of the pattern of black bands and spots produces most of the varieties, but in one of the rarest and most highly prized the copper ground colour is replaced by silvery white.

Large copper

In this species the wing span is about $1\frac{7}{10}$ in. and the male and female are very different. In the male all four wings on the upper side are brilliant burnished copper with only narrow dark borders and small central dots. The female has dark markings not unlike those of the small copper.

The large copper was discovered in Britain a little before 1800, in the fens of East Anglia, a habitat that was rapidly shrinking due to artificial drainage. Butterfly collecting was already a popular pastime, and the coppers were persecuted without restraint. Not only did collectors visit their haunts, but dealers encouraged the local people to capture them in all their stages for sale at prices ranging from a few pence to a shilling, rich rewards for the poor of those days. The butterfly held out for half a cen-

Small copper larvae feed on dock and sorrel.

tury, the last specimens being taken in 1847 or 1848. The British large copper could probably have been saved if a reserve had been created where it could have been secure from the greed of collectors and from destruction of its habitat, but at that time the idea had not occurred to anyone that active measures might be taken to preserve rare animals from extinction.

The large copper is still found in many parts of Europe and Asia, but the British subspecies was larger and finer than any of the Continental forms. About a thousand preserved specimens of it exist, but as a living animal it has gone for ever. The great water dock is the food plant of the large copper. The caterpillar, which is attended

by ants, is green and looks like a much flattened slug. It hibernates when young, feeds in the following spring, and the butterflies appear in July and August.

Two other species, the scarce copper and the purple-edged copper, were included as British by early entomologists. It is not impossible that they once lived in this country and became extinct before collecting became methodical and widespread. Both are well distributed in continental Europe.

Butterfly naturalisation

In 1915 a subspecies of the large copper was discovered in the province of Friesland, Holland, and named *Lycaena dispar batavus*. It resembles the extinct English race more closely than any other and the idea occurred to some British naturalists to try introducing it to the fenland nature reserves in East Anglia. It is rare in its native haunts, and some difficulty was experienced in obtaining living specimens. This was overcome, however, and the first butterflies were released by the Society for the Promotion of Nature Reserves in Wood Walton Fen, Huntingdonshire, in 1927. The experiment was successful and later was repeated at Wicken Fen, owned by the National Trust, in Cambridgeshire. The Dutch large copper

is still maintained at Wood Walton and is bred artificially and released every year to supplement wild stock and to ensure against any accident to the small wild population.

phylum	**Arthropoda**	
class	**Insecta**	
order	**Lepidoptera**	
family	**Lycaenidae**	
genus & species	***Lycaena dispar*** *large copper*	
	L. hippothoe *purple-edged copper*	
	L. phlaeas *small copper*	
	L. virgauteae *scarce copper*	

Coral

Corals are polyps similar to anemones (see p. 128) except that they are supported by a hard chalky skeleton. This, often white when dead, is covered in life with a continuous layer of flesh from which the polyps spring, and the whole is often beautifully coloured. The true corals, or stony corals as they are often called, may be either solitary or colonial. In the first a single polyp lives on its own, seated in a chalky cup or on a mushroom-shaped chalky skeleton. The colonial corals are made up of a sheet of tissue, formed by hundreds or thousands of polyps, covering the chalky skeleton. They may be tree-, cup- or dome-shaped, made up of flattened plates or branching like stag's horns.

There are also soft corals, some of which are precious. They are not true corals. One important difference is that their tentacles, instead of being simple as in the true corals and sea-anemones, are fringed, and each polyp has eight tentacles instead of, as in true corals, six or some multiple of six. Soft corals are usually tree-like and the centres of the stems and branches are strengthened by a chalky material, coloured red or black, and this, stripped of its flesh, gives the precious corals of commerce. Related to the precious corals are the sea-fans, the stems and branches of which are strengthened by a flexible horny material. Another relative is the beautiful organ-pipe coral, a mass of vertical tubes joined at intervals throughout their length by thin horizontal plates. The skeleton is reddish-purple and the polyps a pale lilac. When expanded these look like delicate flowers.

Tropical reef builders

Corals live in all seas, but few are found in temperate and polar regions compared with those found in the tropics—and in particular the reef-builders. Thousands of miles of tropical shores, especially in the Indian Ocean, are edged with reefs. In places, barrier reefs are formed, many miles offshore, like the Great Barrier Reef, which runs for 1 200 miles parallel with the northeast coast of Australia. In mid-ocean, especially in the Pacific, are ring-shaped atolls made of living coral, topping accumulations of dead coral skeletons, which in places go down to about a mile deep.

Birth of a reef

Reef-building corals are found north and south of the equator about as far as the 25th line of latitude, where the temperature of the sea does not fall much below 18°C/65°F. Each begins as a larva which, after swimming about for a while, settles on the bottom and changes into a polyp. A small lump appears on its side. This is a bud. It gets bigger, a mouth appears at its free end and a crown of tentacles grows around the mouth. The bud then continues to grow until it is the same size and shape as the

parent, but without becoming separated from it. By repeated budding of the parent stock, and of the new growths formed from it, a colony numbering sometimes hundreds of thousands is formed. Between them they build a common skeleton, which in the end may be several feet high and the same across. Since all the polyps are in close connection with each other they are fed communally by their many mouths and stomachs.

Living animal traps

Corals, whether solitary, reef or soft, feed like sea-anemones. The tentacles are armed with stinging cells by which small swimming animals are paralysed and then pushed into the mouth at the centre of the ring of tentacles. In reef corals the polyps are withdrawn during the day, so the surface of each coral mass is more or less smooth. As night falls and the plankton animals rise into the surface waters, the polyps and their tentacles become swollen with water drawn in through the mouth by currents set up by cilia on the skin. The polyps now stand out on the surface, their delicate tentacles forming a semi-transparent pile in which are many mouths waiting to receive prey. The seemingly inert coral has been converted into a huge trap for any small animals which pass nearby—underlining the relationship with anemones.

The polyps of some corals have short tentacles, which do not carry food to the mouth. Instead, it is passed to the mouth by the cilia coating the tentacles.

There has always been some doubt, however, whether this was their only method of feeding. In coral tissues live microscopic single-celled plants known as zooxanthellae. It has been supposed that these two, the polyps and the zooxanthellae, were living in symbiosis: that the zooxanthellae received shelter and used the waste products from the coral, while the coral benefited from oxygen given off by its plant guests. Some scientists maintained that in addition the coral fed on the surplus populations of the plants.

This has been disputed, and one reason why it was hard to reach the truth is that digestion is very rapid. Consequently no animal food is found in the coral stomachs by day, therefore it has been assumed that they must be feeding on something else and, so it was argued, they must be eating the zooxanthellae. On the other hand, the tentacles react to animal food only, suggesting that corals are wholly carnivorous. Moreover, if coral polyps are deprived of animal food they soon shrink, showing signs of malnutrition. These are only a few of the arguments and they are enough to indicate the causes of disagreement.

From investigations carried out about 1960 by TF Goreau in the West Indies it seems that the zooxanthellae help the corals to grow by removing carbon dioxide from their tissues. Corals grow best in bright light, less well in dull light when zooxanthellae are fewer, and least of all in darkness when their zooxanthellae have been killed off by lack of sunlight. This alone suggests that there is a close link between the rate of growth of the coral and the presence of tiny plants in its tissues.

Walking corals

The majority of corals are sedentary. The original meaning of this word is 'to sit for long periods', but in zoology it is used more to indicate animals that are permanently fixed to the substratum. There is, however, at least one coral that moves about, but it does not travel under its own steam. It represents a very picturesque example of symbiosis, or living together for mutual benefit.

In October 1967, TF Goreau and Sir Maurice Yonge were exploring the Great Barrier Reef of Australia when they discovered on the lee side of the reef, on a muddy bottom, small corals, less than an inch across, which moved about over the mud. They were able to take some to the laboratory and watch them in an aquarium.

Pollution and the development of tourist resorts are damaging many coral reefs. Being very slow growing, the reefs may take decades or even centuries to recover. Coral reef reserves have now been established in many countries.

Precious corals have long been highly valued as carving materials and for making jewellery. As a consequence, they are now scarce in the Mediterranean and there is concern that precious corals in the Pacific are also under threat.

phylum	**Cnidaria**
class	**Anthozoa**
order	**Scleractinia**
genera	***Fungia, Porites, Heteropsammia*** *others*

▷ *Four examples of dead coral colonies show how they are made up of skeletal frameworks of individual polyps. In life, these skeletons are covered with beautifully-coloured layers of living flesh (see overleaf).*

▽ *Diagram of the basic colony of the* Heliopora *blue coral shows the shape of the hard, chalky skeleton* (in red) *and the polyps which grow from it* (top).

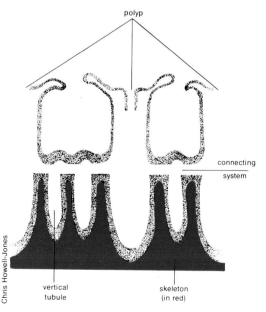

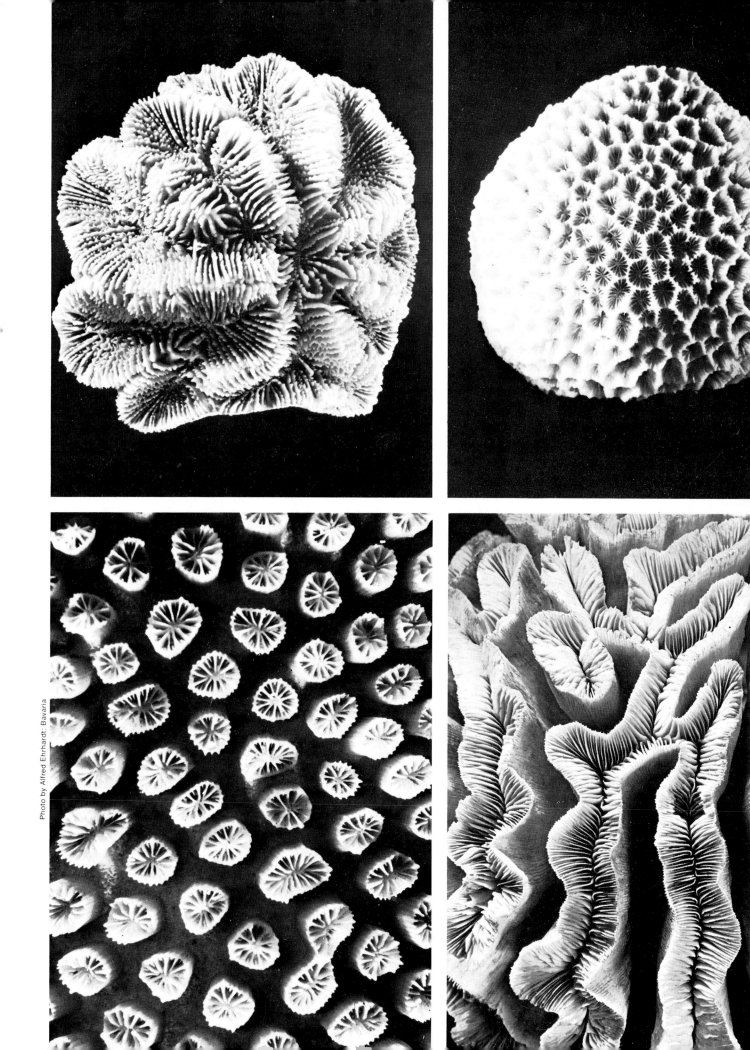

Underwater garden

◁ *This assortment gives a good idea of the different types of coral which will grow side by side to form a coral reef.*

△ *All systems 'go': the polyps of a coral, fully extended while feeding at night.*

◁ *A closer view of feeding polyps of a hard coral show the fine, whiskery tentacles that sweep the surrounding water for food.*

▷ *Living polyps protrude from branches of staghorn coral off Mauritius.*

▷▷ *Unidentified shallow-water coral in the Seychelles has a squat, bunched structure.*

Anthony Bannister: NHPA

Anthony Bannister: NHPA

▷ *Fish swarm around a coral reef precipice in the Red Sea.*

G Mundey

Coral snake

Coral snake is the name given to many strikingly-coloured snakes with patterns of rings running round the body and tail. The body is slender, and there is no pronounced distinction between head and neck, as in the vipers. In North and South America there are several genera of true coral snakes, which are close relatives of the cobras, as are the Oriental coral snakes belonging to the genus Maticora. *In South Africa some members of the genus* Aspidelaps *are called coral snakes, and they are very similar in appearance and habits to their American relatives.*

The two North American coral snakes have prominent rings round the body in the same sequence of black, yellow or white, and red. The Arizona or Sonora coral snake is small, having a maximum recorded length of 19½ in. The larger common coral snake occasionally reaches over 3½ ft. Some tropical species reach 4 or 5 ft.

Brightly-coloured banding is not in-

and to inject a lethal quantity of venom the snake chews the flesh, lacerating the skin and so forcing in a large amount of poison, which acts on the nervous system and has a very powerful effect. In Mexico the common coral snake is called the '20-minute snake' as its bite is supposed to be fatal within that time. But 24 hours is a more likely time. Surprisingly few deaths have been reported.

Coral snakes are nocturnal, lying up during the day in runs under stones or bark or in mossy clumps, but they are sometimes active during the day if it has been raining. They trouble people little because of their secretive habits. When man is abroad during the day, coral snakes are resting away from the danger of being trodden on, which would cause them to bite. Occasionally there are reports of coral snake bites but these are usually due to people carelessly handling them.

Snake eaters

The jaws of coral snakes do not open very wide and they can eat only slender prey, which consists mainly of small lizards, other snakes and probably insects.

swallowed the bullfrog, it is strange that it was not able either to escape or to poison its adversary.

First-class animal puzzle

Parallels can be drawn between the brightly-coloured coral snake, perhaps the most gaudy of animals, apart from some of the birds and fishes, and the bright stripes of bees and wasps. Conspicuous colouring is a feature of many animals that are poisonous.

In the insect world, some harmless insects, such as hoverflies, mimic the colour patterns of the harmful bees and wasps, gaining protection because birds and other predators learn to connect the colour with an unpleasant taste. It is suggested that the coral snakes also have their mimics, for in America, Africa and Asia there are non-poisonous snakes with brightly-coloured rings. In the United States some reports of coral snakes in unusual places have been due to two non-poisonous snakes, the scarlet snake and the scarlet king snake. These, however, have a different sequence of bands. In the coral snakes the red band has yellow or white on either side. In the mimics the red band has a black band on either side. This is put another way by Drs Boys and Smith in their book on recognising poisonous amphibians and reptiles and treating their bites:
'Red on yellow (or white)
Kill a fellow (or might);
Red on black
Venom lack'
This distinction does not hold elsewhere in America. The false coral snake of South America has yellow bands.

The trouble with the theory of the coral snake's bright colours being a warning is that it is nocturnal, so enemies are unlikely to see the colour and therefore are unlikely to learn that a bright-banded snake is dangerous. How then are the mimicking snakes, who are also secretive, to profit? One habit shared by many ringed snakes, both venomous and harmless, is to coil themselves up with the head underneath and wave the tail, which looks rather like the head in these species. Perhaps this leads an enemy to attack a less vulnerable part of the snake. However, one animal who does notice bright colour is man, and because he will kill any snake that might be poisonous, the harmless mimics actually suffer from looking like a venomous snake.

It has been suggested that the banding on coral snakes, perhaps also on their mimics, is in the nature of a disruptive pattern, breaking up the outline of the body, so making the animal less readily seen by predators. This still leaves unexplained the presence of typical warning colours in the patterns.

Technicolor warning technique. Bright colours do for the coral what the dry, sinister rattle does for the rattlesnake: they warn potential attackers not to try their luck.

John Tashjian at Fort Worth Zoo

variable in coral snakes. The genus Leptomicrurus *has long thin bodies and short tails, which are dark on the upper side and have yellow spots underneath.*

Of the many species of New World coral snakes, only two extend as far north as the United States. The common coral snake extends north from Mexico, through eastern Texas to the low-lying country of Kentucky and North Carolina and south to Florida. The Arizona coral snake lives in the arid lands of Arizona, New Mexico and northern Mexico. Other coral snakes range south to northern Argentina.

Poisonous but rarely dangerous

Coral snakes do not strike like a cobra, but approach their victim slowly, sliding their head over its flesh. The fangs are short

Breeding

The common coral snake lays 3–14 soft, elongated eggs in May or June, in a hollow in the earth or under a log. When they hatch, after 10–12 weeks, the young snakes measure 7–8 in. and have pale skins, the colours of which become more intense as they get older.

Enemies

Snake-eaters themselves, coral snakes are preyed upon by other snake-eaters such as the king snake, which is resistant to the effects of coral snake venom. On Trinidad, mongooses, which were introduced to keep down the numbers of snakes, have not affected the coral snake population.

One unusual report is that of a large bullfrog eating a 17in. coral snake. Although the narrow-jawed snake could not have

class	**Reptilia**
order	**Squamata**
suborder	**Serpentes**
family	**Elapidae**
genera	*Micruroides*
	Micrurus
	Leptomicrurus
	others

Cormorant

Cormorant and shag are names applied indiscriminately to the 30 species of the family Phalacrocoracidae. Only in the British Isles does each name refer to a certain species, where cormorant describes the common cormorant, and shag the green cormorant. The common cormorant, the largest of all, is also known as the great cormorant in North America and the black cormorant in Australia and New Zealand. The plumage is generally glossy black with some bronze and an overall greyish appearance to the head and neck due to some greyish-white feathers. There is a characteristic white patch on the chin and sides of the face. The shag has a glossy bottle-green plumage and is distinguished from the common cormorant by the absence of white on the head and by having a small, curved crest during the breeding season, which is, however, a feature of many other members of the family.

The various species of cormorant are best identified by the shape and colouring of the patch of naked skin on the face, although these variations can only be detected at close quarters. Brandt's cormorant, the commonest species on the Pacific coast of North America, has blue patches, and the double-crested cormorant, the commonest elsewhere in North America, has orange-yellow patches. The face patches of the Magellan cormorant are red. Many of the species living in the southern hemisphere have white, rather than mainly dark, underparts.

Cosmopolitan swimmers

Cormorants are found all over the world except on the islands of the central Pacific. The pelagic cormorant is found in the Bering Sea, while, to the south, the blue-eyed shag, named for its ultramarine eyes surrounded by rings of blue naked skin, breeds on islands off the west coast of the Antarctic Peninsula.

Although the webbed feet, upright stance and long neck all suggest an aquatic life, cormorants are rarely found far out to sea. Most of them live by shallow coastal waters, or inland on lakes and rivers. The most cosmopolitan species is the common cormorant which is found over most of Europe, Asia, Africa, Australasia and eastern North America. The most restricted is the flightless cormorant that breeds on two islands only of the Galapagos. This is one of the largest cormorants. It has completely lost the power of flight and has paralleled the penguins in its flipper-like wings and dense hair-like plumage. Another cormorant that could fly only weakly was Pallas' cormorant which was discovered on the Komandorski Islands by Steller and Bering when they were marooned there in 1741. A century later it was extinct.

Other cormorants are strong fliers, keeping aloft on rapid wingbeats with neck stretched out. They will also soar in air currents, but usually they fly low over the

△ An obliging duo show both the cormorant's basic streamline and its characteristic stance.

▽ A mixed bag. Cormorants share a nesting site with a group of sacred ibis.

Stephen Dalton: NHPA

Des Bartlett: Photo Res

Two generations — fledgeling and adult blue-eyed shags in southern waters, with nesting chinstrap penguins.

surface of the water. All of them swim well, floating low in the water, sometimes with only head and neck showing. To submerge, they either duck-dive, jumping up and plunging in head-first, or merely sink beneath the surface. The longest recorded dive is of 71 seconds and cormorants may go down as far as 100 ft. Normally they stay under for less than half a minute, swimming about 20–30 ft below the surface.

Fishing in flocks

Except for a few crustaceans, such as crabs, molluscs and occasionally frogs and reptiles, cormorants feed on fish. The flightless cormorant feeds on octopus and fish, mainly eels, which it finds in great numbers around its home islands, where the cool Humboldt current wells up and mixes with the warm equatorial waters to form a fertile area with an abundance of plankton and fish.

The British cormorant and shag have slightly different diets. The cormorant feeds mainly on bottom-living fish such as flat fish and sand eels while the shag eats eels and fish from the middle and upper waters. In this way the two closely-related species that nest on the same cliffs, and fish in the same waters, do not compete for food.

Flocks of cormorants go out feeding together. They can be seen flying in lines then settling on the water, gathering in a tight bunch. They swim about, lowering their heads into the water to look for fish, then one dives and the others follow it. Flocks of little black cormorants are reported to locate shoals of fish then swim round them in decreasing circles to concentrate them and double-crested cormorants have been seen driving shoals of fish up a bay into shallower water.

Fish are brought to the surface, to be

swallowed head first. Large fish are shaken or beaten against the water until their struggles weaken. This habit has been used by Japanese fishermen, who train cormorants to bring their catch back to the boat. Leather collars are used to prevent the cormorants from swallowing the catch.

Other fishermen persecute the cormorant for its fish-eating habits, but the cormorants' gluttony has given rise to an important industry. The guanay of Peru and Chile and the cape cormorant of South Africa feed in vast numbers, and their droppings, deposited on the breeding grounds, form guano. This is dug out and used as a very rich fertilizer.

Nesting on rocks and in trees

Cormorants nest in colonies varying from a few pairs, perhaps only one or two in the case of the king cormorant of the Falkland

A trio of shags limber up their long, sinuous necks, much used in courtship. Moulting chinstrap penguin at right.

Islands, to thousands of pairs of guanays. The colonies are usually situated on rocky cliffs and the nests may be within a few feet of each other. Other colonies, especially those inland, may be in dead trees. The nest is a bowl of twigs, grasses, reeds or seaweed, which becomes plastered with the birds' droppings.

Courtship displays—the flightless cormorants' may take place in the water—involve much waving of the long neck. In soliciting, the female bends her neck right over her back.

The 2–4 eggs are incubated by both parents. The chicks hatch in 3–5 weeks. At first they are naked and have skins like black leather. Later they grow a curly, dark grey down. The parents feed them on fish, which the chicks take by pushing their heads down the parent's gullet. The chicks leave the nest in 5–8 weeks.

In peril at sea

The colonies are usually hard to get at, and by nesting on cliffs or in trees, cormorants are safe from enemies on land; but they sometimes get caught at sea. A humpback whale has been found dead with a cormorant stuck in its throat, having swallowed six others; and an angler fish that caught one was carried to the surface by the cormorant's buoyancy, but not in time to save the bird. Pike and cod have also been found with the remains of cormorants in their stomachs and leopard seals are known to chase them.

The blue-eyed shags of the sub-Antarctic seas face another problem. Dominican gulls have learned to wait by the flocks of feeding shags and steal the fish as the cormorants bring them to the surface. Sometimes the gulls dive in and intercept the shags as they are surfacing.

Cormorants keep their distance

Anyone who knows cormorants is familiar with the way they perch with wings held fully outspread. The generally accepted explanation is that the cormorant, that spends so much of its time in the water, is hanging out its wings to dry. It has been suggested that this is necessary because their wings are not very well waterproofed. Yet this would be most surprising in a family of birds who are not only aquatic themselves, but whose relatives such as pelicans, boobies and gannets are also aquatic. No other aquatic birds—except darters—hang their wings out to dry, and, furthermore, close observation does not suggest that standing with wings spread is connected with drying. Cormorants can be seen holding their wings open in pouring rain, when drying is im-

Graham Pizzey: NHPA

Apart from the seas of the central Pacific, cormorants have a worldwide range stretching from Greenland to the sub-Antarctic islands. They will also frequent suitable stretches of water inland, the exception here being the northern Asian land mass.

John Tashjian at San Diego Zoo

possible, or after they have flown from one perch to another, when drying is not necessary. On other occasions they may come out of the sea and perch with wings folded.

Cormorants habitually perch a short distance from each other, so a group of them on a rock are evenly spaced out in a line. When another bird lands, it extends its wings and its neighbours shift away. Then the newcomer folds its wings and the line of cormorants is still well-spaced with a wingspan between each one. So it seems that wing-spreading is a device that helps to keep individuals apart, for no animal likes being cheek by jowl with its neighbour. In sociable species, rituals are needed to promote harmony between individuals (see discussion on allopreening under avadavat, p 106) and courtship displays of birds reduce aggression and fear between the pair.

There may be another function. When they are frightened they suddenly fly off together, lumbering into the air with laboured wing beats. To make a clean getaway it is necessary to avoid collisions with neighbouring birds. Therefore, being spaced out is an advantage in a quick takeoff.

class	**Aves**
order	**Pelecaniformes**
family	**Phalacrocoracidae**
genera & species	***Phalacrocorax carbo*** *common cormorant* ***P. aristotelis*** *shag, others* ***Halietor pygmaeus*** *pigmy cormorant, others* ***Nannopterum harrisi*** *flightless cormorant*

Left: Pied cormorant and chick on the Abrolhos Islands, western Australia. Below: In captivity: flightless cormorant from the Galapagos Islands in the San Diego zoo. Although their wings are quite useless for flight, these cormorants adopt their flying relatives' typical 'wings-akimbo' stance. Right: Cormorant colonies usually nest on rocky cliffs within a few feet of each other, but some colonies—especially inland ones—will build nests in dead trees.

Atlas Vienne: Bavaria

Found throughout in suitable habitats

Common cormorant *(Phalacrocorax carbo)*

Corncrake

Also called the land rail, the corncrake is a member of the rail family and is related to the coot and moorhen, which it resembles in form, although it is slightly smaller. It lives more on land than other rails. The plumage is yellowish-buff, marked with black on the upper parts, and greyish on head and breast. The wings are a rusty-red, very conspicuous when the bird is in flight.

Victims of progress

The corncrake breeds in Europe and Central Asia, from the south of Norway, Sweden and Finland to the Mediterranean coast, excluding Spain, Italy, Greece and the Balkans. During years of warm weather it extends its range northwards, but, overall, its range has decreased during this century. Originally agriculture helped the spread of the corncrake, for it is a bird of grassland, but now mechanical mowers have acted against it. At the turn of the century corncrakes were common over the British Isles. Now they are abundant only in the wilder parts of Western Ireland, the Hebrides, Orkney and Shetland, while a few breed regularly in some places on the mainland of Scotland and North Wales, all areas where there is little intensive agriculture.

Corncrakes are migratory, wintering in southern Asia and Africa, as far south as South Africa. Asian corncrakes reach Australia on very rare occasions. When flushed, corncrakes fly feebly, with legs dangling, so that it would seem strange that they can undertake long migrations. When on migration, however, the flight is steadier and more determined, but they fly near the ground and another possible cause of their decline is that they often run into overhead wires and cables.

Even where it is common, the corncrake is rarely seen because it is most active during the evening, when it skulks in the cover of vegetation, taking off only when alarmed. Nevertheless, its presence is well-advertised by the monotonous, two-beat call of the male which is kept up for hours on end both by day and night. The call is described as a creaking and can be imitated by running a piece of wood over the teeth of a comb.

Feeding

Corncrakes live on a variety of foods, mainly animal, and mostly insects such as beetles, earwigs, weevils and flies, including eggs and larvae as well as adults. Slugs and snails, earthworms, millipedes and spiders are eaten in smaller quantities. Plant food includes seeds, grains and some greenery.

Mother shoulders burden of family

The migrants reach the British Isles from their winter quarters in mid-April—mid-May. The males begin to call a few days after their arrival and continue for 2–3 weeks, stopping when the eggs are laid. They may start again after hatching and can be heard until late August, about a month before they migrate south again.

The male displays to the female with head held low, wings spread so the tips just touch the ground, and the feathers of the neck and sides fluffed out to form a ruff. He circles round her, moving his head from side to side and she turns all the time to keep facing him until mating.

The eggs, 6–14, are laid in a flat pad of plucked grass among grass, nettles, low undergrowth or in cereal crops. Low-lying water meadows seem to be preferred, but in upland areas corncrakes are found in pastures and crofts. The eggs are incubated by the female for 14–15 days. As she does

The wedge-shaped, elusive corncrake or land rail is on the decline in Britain. Once the spread of agriculture caused it to thrive, but now one of its most potent enemies is the combine harvester.

not start incubation until the last egg is laid, all hatch out within 24 hours. For about 4 days the chicks are fed by the female or by both parents. After that they can run about with the parents, feeding themselves. They start to fly when 5 weeks old, but cannot fly well for another 2 or 3 weeks.

Advancing agriculture defeats corncrakes

The downfall of the corncrake was brought about by the introduction of mowing machines and the progressive bringing forward of the hay-cutting season, so the date for haymaking coincided with the birds' nesting. This led to the destruction of eggs and young chicks. In Holland, at least, the corncrakes were able to avoid this to some extent by moving into cornfields, but this is only a temporary respite as there

is a similar trend for early harvesting of cereal crops.

In the British Isles, corncrakes began to decrease in the last quarter of the 19th century. They had never been common in many parts of East Anglia, but in 1875 it was noticed that fewer were nesting in Middlesex and the last record of nesting was in 1926. The decline spread northwards and westwards, although in the early parts of this century corncrakes could still be heard in Richmond Park, Kew Gardens, and on Wimbledon Common. The last strongholds in the British Isles began to fall after the Second World War, when mechanisation of agriculture reached the Scottish islands and the western side of Ireland. In the Shetland Islands the crofters used to leave the grass surrounding nests uncut; or if there were young these would be removed to the side of the field. Now mowing machines are used they still try to avoid the nests but these are usually too well camouflaged and cannot be seen in time. Their best chances of survival occur when the weather is bad and the harvest late.

class	**Aves**
order	**Gruiformes**
family	**Rallidae**
genus & species	***Crex crex***

Cotinga

Many of the cotingas have ornate plumage with brilliant colours, as well as crests, wattles and other adornments, while others such as the tityras and the becards are plainer. Only males are showy; the females are usually drab and inconspicuous. There are about 90 species in the family, which differ so widely in form that they were once placed in several families. The masked tityra is a 7in. long bird with black head and wings and grey body. The white-winged becard, although dull in colour, is still very pretty. The male is black on the upper parts with a grey rump and white wing patches. The female is olive-green above and pale yellow below. More ornate is the Pompadour cotinga with its lavender plumage and white wings. The female is grey. The Pompadour cotinga was named after Madame de Pompadour, by a British ornithologist, as the specimens he received were from a captured cargo ship on its way to France, where the cotinga feathers would have been used in the millinery made famous by the French courtesan.

The name cotinga comes from the Amazon Indian word for washed white and originally described the white bellbird, or snowy cotinga. A near relative is the three-wattled bellbird. This has reddish-brown plumage with a white head and chest and three whip-like wattles dangling from the base of the beak.

The two most ornate cotingas are the cock-of-the-rock (see p. 604) and the umbrella bird which are treated under separate headings.

Cotingas are mainly birds of the dense forests in the Amazon basin, but they spread south to the northern borders of Argentina and north through Central America to the borders of the United States, living in pine and deciduous forests of high country and the bushy edges of forests as well as in the rain forests. One species, the Jamaican becard, has reached the West Indies, where it lives in the highlands of Jamaica.

Mystery voices

There are almost as many different ways of life as there are different body forms of the cotingas, living in the upper layers of foliage of dense forests. They are united in one family by their remarkable voices. It is for their persistent calling that they are best known. To the bird watcher fighting his way through the undergrowth the calls may be the only sign of cotingas which are flitting about in the dense greenery high overhead. The bellbirds, for instance, like the other birds in Australia and New Zealand that have the same name, produce loud, bell-like peals that can be heard a mile or so away. The calf or capuchin bird, chestnut brown with black tail and wings and a bare blue-grey patch of skin on its face, makes a mooing or grunting call. The

Naked-throated bellbird

E Lindsey

669

Popperfoto

△ *The three-wattled bellbird sports three slim wattles sprouting from the base of its bill.*

TW Roth Photo Res

△ *Rieffer's cotinga. The cotinga family is mostly confined to the tropical forests of central and South America, but some species have spread to the southern borders of the USA and to the Caribbean.*

tityras also 'grunt' in a most unbirdlike manner. Other cotingas are less vocal, some having very quiet songs. The white-winged becard, however, is a notable songster, singing from March to September. It has a special dawn song that can be heard, almost. without a break, for an hour after sunrise.

Feeding

Many cotingas are fruit eaters, but some eat a proportion of insects. The tityras which have hooked, shrike-like bills will catch dragonflies and lizards, and the white-winged becards have been seen flying up to foliage and picking insects off without landing.

Elaborate courtship and hidden nests

In keeping with their brilliant plumage, the male cotingas often have elaborate courtship rituals. After courtship and mating the females rear the families on their own. The climax of courtship displays in the cotingas is reached by the cock-of-the-rock (see p 472) when several males gather in one place to display. Other cotingas have special grounds but they display alone. The bearded bellbird courts and mates on a special branch, as does the capuchin bird which clears its branch of twigs by neatly snapping them off with its bill.

The less brilliant cotingas have a more formal married life. The tityras remain paired the whole year round and although the male does not help with nest-building or the incubation of the two eggs he will fly about with the female, keeping her company. Similarly, the male white-winged becard sings to his mate while she builds the nest. This is a bulky construction, built high in the treetops with a doorway in the side. The 3 or 4 eggs are incubated for 18–19 days, and the male helps to feed the fledglings which stay in the nest for 21 days.

The masked tityra makes her nest in a

hole, usually one abandoned by a wood-pecker, as much as 100 ft up. The nest is made by dropping dead leaves and twiglets, plucked from nearby branches, into the cavity. More material may be added during incubation. As tityra nests are usually high in trees that are often very rotten, few observations have been made on them and the incubation period is unknown. Alexander Skutch, a well-known American ornithologist, once managed to climb up to the nest of a masked tityra but he said that he did so only when enthusiasm overruled judgement and that he did not advise it as a pastime. In this case the tree stood in deep water behind a dam and was consequently very rotten, but Dr Skutch decided it was worth the attempt because if something snapped and he fell, landing in water was better than landing on land. With the aid of a ladder and the encouragement of his companion he reached the nest to find a hollow, 1 ft deep, with an inch layer of leaf fragments on which two coffee-coloured eggs lay.

Enemies take over their nests

Cotinga nests may be destroyed by the nest-robbing toucans called araçaris, but sometimes tityras have been found successfully rearing broods in the same trees that the araçaris were using. Parasitic flycatchers have been known to destroy becard nests and to rear their own families in them, and a species of large black bee will do likewise, blocking up the nest entrance with wax.

Crowding the neighbours

Not all birds that live in holes are able to excavate their own. Like some mammals that live in others' burrows, they nest in cavities abandoned by woodpeckers and others. The tityras go even further: they oust the rightful owners by haunting the nest-hole and making a nuisance of themselves until

the owners are forced to move. This is because the tityras, although normally mild-mannered, refuse to relinquish a hole once they have set their hearts on it. At first they probably claim it, in all innocence, while the owner is away. They then start to bring nesting material and drop it into the cavity. At first there is retaliation, and the woodpeckers or toucans that first had the hole remove the leaf litter that the tityras bring in. The tityras, however, appear to win through sheer persistence. While the other birds are away during the day the tityras can accumulate a good pile of leaves. Dr Skutch relates how three araçaris that shared a hole for roosting had difficulty squeezing into it, because of the material brought in by a pair of tityras. They had to abandon the normal method of entering headfirst and turn around for the more awkward method of backing in with tail doubled over. Sometimes they could not all get in and one or two had to sleep elsewhere. The tityras were now firmly convinced to whom the hole belonged and attacked the much larger araçaris as they tried to get in, and, luckily for them, the latter eventually gave up and moved to a hole that did not shrink every day.

class	**Aves**
order	**Passeriformes**
family	**Cotingidae**
genera & species	***Procnias averano*** *bearded bellbird* ***P. tricarunculata*** *three-wattled bellbird* ***Tityra semifasciata*** *masked tityra* ***Xipholena punicea*** *Pompadour cotinga* *others*

Caught by the camera: a cottontail surprised while resting prepares to make itself scarce. These rabbits fall prey to every flesh-eater in their region, and often need all their flashing speed to escape.

Cottontail

The cottontail is a small rabbit varying from dark grey to reddish-brown. The upper parts are brown and sides grey, with a rufous nape and legs. The ears are short and rounded. The tail is brown above and white below and gives rise to the name cottontail from its resemblance to a cotton boll. There are about 13 species whose head and body length varies from 10 – 18 in. and weight from 14 oz – 5 lb.

Abundant everywhere

Cottontail rabbits of various kinds range from southern Canada to South America, as far as Argentina and Paraguay. Over this range they live in a wide variety of habitats. Most species prefer open woodland and brush or clearings in forests. Consequently some species flourished in early colonial times when European settlers were first opening up the forests. Later, complete destruction of forests acted against these species. The New England cottontail of the Appalachians preferred open woodland with undergrowth, but with the spread of agriculture this species has been replaced by the Eastern cottontail that inhabits open country such as pastureland.

Other species of cottontail live in more extreme habitats. The smallest species, the Idaho cottontail, lives in deserts, and the largest, the swamp or marsh rabbit, sometimes called the 'canecutter', lives in swampy areas. It has large feet with splayed, slightly furred toes, and swims well. When alarmed it is said to make for water where it hides with only nose and ears showing.

Cottontails are timid animals, ready to bolt for cover at the slightest hint of danger, finding a suitable place where they crouch motionless, their neutral colour blending in so well with the vegetation that they are very difficult to find. In this they are aided by their nocturnal habits. Most species are active when the light is dim, but during the summer months, when nights are short, the cottontails are more active and are more likely to be seen in broad daylight.

Each cottontail has a range of several acres that is crossed by regular runs through the ground vegetation. In these runs the animal knows its way so well that it can hurtle at a full speed of 20 – 25 mph when frightened. Cottontails usually use the burrows of other animals, such as woodchucks. Only the Idaho cottontail makes its own burrow.

Making the most of their food

Cottontails eat grass and broad-leaved annuals and can severely damage crops and gardens. The damage is made the more severe because more plants are injured than eaten. Some are trampled and others only nibbled, sufficient to spoil them as a food crop without satisfying the cottontail's hunger. If this is done to young plants they grow stunted and deformed. In winter the cottontails feed on buds and soft twigs, and young saplings can be found neatly cut off at the level of the snowline.

Digestion of coarse herbage and twigs is difficult, as they contain large quantities of indigestible cellulose, which has to be assimilated. Other grazing animals, such as cows and sheep, chew the cud, a process in which food first goes to the rumen, the first compartment of the multiple stomach, where the cellulose is broken down, then brought up to the mouth and back to the true stomach. In rabbits another process is used. Food is passed through the digestive system twice, to ensure complete digestion, by eating the faeces containing food undigested after the first time through.

Breeding like other rabbits

The breeding season is long, from February to September in temperate parts of North America, but in arid areas such as the Sierra Nevada it starts earlier, for in summer the vegetation will have shrivelled and there will be little food for the young. In some parts where conditions are always favourable, breeding may take place all the year round.

Fighting sometimes occurs between males, with fur flying, and courtship dances may take place in which one rabbit leaps in the air while the other runs under it. After mating the male is driven away and the female rears the litter alone. The young cottontails, called fawns, are born a month after mating, naked and blind. There may be up to seven of them, weighing less than 1 oz each. They are placed in a shallow nest that the mother has scraped in the ground, perhaps by enlarging the hoofprint of a horse or cow, and lined with grass and fur plucked from her breast. When she leaves the nest she carefully covers it with grass. The nest is so small that the mother cannot lie in it. Instead she crouches over it and the fawns have to climb up to suckle.

When a fortnight old the fawns leave the nest and feed nearby during the day. They finally disperse when 3 weeks old. Their mother will have mated again within a few hours of their birth and the next litter will soon be due. She may have up to 5 litters in a year.

Every man's meat

Cottontails fall prey to every flesh-eating animal. Skunks, foxes and crows search out and kill the young in the nests and owls, hawks, snakes and chickarees take the young when they leave their nests. Other predators such as bobcats and eagles take the adults. Man also hunts and traps cottontails and in the eastern United States they are the chief game animal, sometimes several million cottontails being killed annually in one State. Their fur is of little use except in the manufacture of felt, but they are eaten, although care is needed in handling and cooking them as a rabbit, disease called turalemia is infectious to man. Proper cooking is sufficient to kill all germs.

Ample food for all

The cottontail, whose only defence is not to be seen as it crouches motionless, half hidden by greenery, forms the staple food of many American predators, much in the same way as the European rabbit once was the mainstay of many carnivores and birds of prey on the other side of the Atlantic. The importance of the cottontail in the natural economy has been shown in studies of the feeding habits of the predators.

One method of finding out an animal's food preferences is to examine the undigested remains passed out in the excrement. Bones of small mammals and birds are often easily identifiable, and while fishes' bones are usually digested, their earbones, or otoliths, may pass through unchanged. The shells of snails and other molluscs may also be present, along with feathers and fur. This method has to be used carefully because it can give misleading results. For instance, fish remains are rarely found around herons' nests because the bones are so easily digested.

In a study made in the Sierra Nevada, cottontails were found to be the staple diet of coyotes, grey foxes, bobcats, horned owls and gopher snakes. The horned owl's diet consisted of 61% cottontails. Rattlesnakes and red-tailed hawks also took large numbers of cottontails, but preferred ground squirrels. These predators are only the main natural enemies of cottontails in this region, and, as well as other animals which take cottontails only occasionally, we must add man, floods and disease as agents that significantly reduce their numbers.

The point of cataloguing the sources of dangers to cottontails is to demonstrate the vast numbers of cottontails that must exist. In the study of the predators' feeding preferences it was calculated that they captured over 7 lb of cottontails each year on every acre of ground. So more than the actual cottontail population is being eaten by only some of their enemies, but the apparent contradiction is solved by the extremely rapid rate of breeding. Each female cottontail is producing litters, averaging four young, 3—5 times a year. If those struck down by a predator only weigh 1 lb, there is still a good surplus left to continue the species.

The cottontail's watchword: run for your life

Photos by L. Lee Rue III: Photo Res.

class	**Mammalia**
order	**Lagomorpha**
family	**Leporidae**
genus	*Sylvilagus*

△ *Getaway: surprised from the rear, a cottontail erupts from a hollow in the snow.* △ *Hotly pursued by a labouring beagle, this cottontail has a good chance of escape.* ▽ *After clearing the snow off its front doorstep, a cottontail surveys the scene.*

Coucal

Despite being members of the cuckoo family, coucals do not lay their eggs in other birds' nests, but make their own. There are about 27 species which are large by cuckoo standards. The pheasant coucal or swamp cuckoo of Australia is 23 in. long with the long tail, characteristic of the cuckoo family, exaggerated to give it a pheasant-like appearance. The tail and rump are a glossy greenish-black, barred with brown and white, while the rest of the plumage is brown or buff with black bars. In the breeding season the male's plumage becomes glossy green-black on the head, neck and underparts.

According to some authorities, the couas of Madagascar belong to the same sub-family as the coucals. They are very similar to the coucals both in form and habit, but there are only about 10 species, compared with the coucal's 27.

Wary bush fowls

Coucals are found in Africa, from Somalia and Senegal to the Cape, as well as in Asia and Australia, reaching as far east as the Solomon Islands. Although widespread and not uncommon in some places, they are not very well known because of their shy habits. Many coucals, including the pheasant coucal and the black coucal, live in swampy country. They prefer to lurk in thick cover, flying as little as possible. The black coucal of central Africa is very difficult to flush once disturbed, and the Senegal coucal hops from bough to bough through bushes, flapping clumsily across open spaces. The blue-headed coucal, however, can often be seen in the morning and evening when it sits on tops of reeds and high grass.

Being so secretive in their habits, coucals are best known by their calls. Many have bubbling calls sounding like water being poured from a bottle. Others have a whooping call, from which the name coucal is derived. The blue-headed coucal has a low 'cou-cou-cou' which is immediately answered by its mate, the call and answer being used to keep in touch while moving about in thick undergrowth. The white-browed coucal also 'bubbles', a pair singing duets in which one bird sings at a higher pitch. It also has a harsh 'chak' call. This is heard especially during and after rain, and as a result this bird has become known as the rainbird in parts of Africa.

Diet of small animals

The blue-headed coucal has the most liberal diet. It feeds on insects, hunts small birds, lizards and reptiles and is also a scavenger. The white-browed coucal that sometimes lives in gardens or fields takes large numbers of grasshoppers and snails as well as snakes and other vertebrates. The pheasant coucal robs nests and occasionally takes to raiding chicken runs. It also kills mice and other small mammals.

▷ *A pheasant coucal feeds its chicks. In this species the cuckoo-like long tail is exaggerated.*

John Warham

674

African relative: the Senegal coucal. The coucals tend to build well-camouflaged nests near the ground, in low bushes or grass clumps. Poor fliers, they spend much of their time on the ground.

Peter Johnson

Well hidden nests

Nests are well camouflaged and built near the ground, in a low bush or tussock of grass. The pheasant coucal's nest is built in a large tussock by drawing the tops of the grass stems together to make a hollow of 4in. diameter, lined with green leaves. It has an opening at either end and the coucal sits on the eggs with head and long tail protruding. Sometimes these nests have an entrance tunnel, also lined with green leaves, which are replaced as they dry out and turn brown. Pheasant coucals have been known, although rarely, to make their nests in deserted babblers' nests.

Both sexes incubate 3–5 eggs for a fortnight. The chicks take about 20 days to fledge. The white-browed coucal is reported to carry its young, one at a time, between its thighs when danger threatens, as from a forest fire. Woodcocks are well known for this behaviour and it is likely

that when all the coucals have been better studied it will be found that other species do the same.

An uneatable pheasant

The common coucal of southeast Asia is known in Malaya and India as the large crow pheasant. As with the pheasant coucal of Australia, the name refers to its long pheasant-like tail feathers. In Malaya the coucal's large size and chestnut and black plumage make it look even more like a pheasant as it runs through the undergrowth or flies heavily across open spaces. As a result inexperienced hunters are likely to shoot in error. An even worse mistake is made if the proud hunter carries it home and persuades his wife that it would make a welcome addition to the menu. Coucal does not resemble pheasant in taste. It is quite uneatable. Even the forest

dwelling aborigines of Malaya, who will eat practically anything else, balk at eating coucal.

It would be interesting to know whether other flesh-eating animals find coucals distasteful. If they did, it would be of great value as a protection from enemies. One meal convinces any human hunter of the futility of hunting coucals; and so, for the sacrifice of a few coucals, the remainder would be safe from non-human enemies who had learned their error.

class	**Aves**
order	**Cuculiformes**
family	**Cuculidae**
genus & species	***Centropus phasianus*** *pheasant coucal* ***C. superciliosus*** *white-browed coucal* ***C. sinensis*** *crow pheasant, others*

675

Courser

Together with the pratincoles, the nine coursers form a family of long-legged, plover-like shorebirds. The most familiar to ornithologists is the cream-coloured courser, a starling-sized bird. It is a pale sandy colour, with creamy legs, distinctive black primary wing feathers and a broad, black and white eye stripe. Temminck's, Burchell's and the Indian coursers are rather similar, but the plumage is much darker. The Australian courser is known to the Australians, incorrectly, as a dotterel. The Egyptian plover, also misnamed, is different from the others. It is a beautiful grey and white with black and green markings.

Coursers live in the Old World from Africa to Australia, six of the nine species breeding in Africa. The cream-coloured courser breeds from the Cape Verde Islands to Persia and south to Kenya. It is a familiar bird of the fringes of the Sahara and occasionally wanders north into Europe. It has occasionally been seen in the British Isles. Of the two Indian species Jerdon's courser is probably extinct. The last record was in 1900.

Desert runners

As their name suggests, coursers are good runners and, like many birds that have specialised in running, they have lost the fourth, backward-facing toe. Although they can fly well, some migrating considerable distances, they can usually only be forced to take off if chased very hard.

Coursers generally live in dry sandy places or in grassland, the exception being the Egyptian plover which lives along sandy river banks, and Temminck's courser which lives in woods and forests where there are open spaces.

Outside the breeding season coursers gather in small parties. As they run about, they have the habit of stopping to stretch up on tiptoe and crane their necks to peer around them. When frightened they crouch down to conceal themselves against the ground, rather than take flight.

Feeding

Coursers live mainly on insects such as beetles, grasshoppers, ants, flies and caterpillars, but they also eat snails and occasionally small lizards.

Eggs are watered to keep cool

As a rule, coursers do not make a nest, laying their two or three eggs on the bare ground, but Temminck's courser and the Australian dotterel sometimes make a depression in the ground. The eggs are incubated, or shielded from the sun, by the female alone. The Egyptian plover broods its eggs during the night when the air and soil surface cool down rapidly, while in the daytime it covers the eggs with sand to prevent them from getting too hot.

Neither the length of the incubation period nor the time the young spend with their parents are known. They can run very

Peter Johnson

△ *Stolid parent: a courser squats on its eggs. Coursers do not usually build nests, but lay their eggs on the bare ground; although sometimes they will make a small hollow to lay in.*

▽ *A black-backed courser cleans its bill. Long-legged, plover-like shorebirds, coursers are good runners, and have lost the normal backward-facing toe in their evolution.*

Constance P Warner

676

shortly after hatching, but are shaded from the sun by each parent in turn during the middle of the day. The Egyptian plover also buries its chicks, partially or completely, as with the eggs. Chicks have been found an inch or more under the surface, which is sufficient to protect them from the worst of the heat, while not being too deep to prevent them from breathing. Furthermore, the parents cool the sand by fetching water from a nearby river and regurgitating it over the place where the chicks are buried.

Another habit of the Egyptian plover, and of the Australian dotterel, and, for all we know, of other coursers, is to hastily bury their chicks if danger threatens. The chicks flatten themselves against the ground, if possible in a small depression. Hippopotamus footprints have been described as being a suitable hiding place. The adult then hastily kicks sand over the crouching chicks and makes its own escape, running away and luring the enemy from the chicks.

The crocodile's toothpick

If the Egyptian plover's parental behaviour is not sufficient to brand it as a bird with unusual habits the story of the crocodile bird, dating from the Greeks, will confirm it.

The crocodile bird, or trochilus as it was then called, was supposed to enter a crocodile's mouth as it lay basking with its mouth open to pick pieces of meat from between its teeth and leeches from its gums. The Elizabethan writers, notably John Leo, told how the trochilus avoided being eaten by pricking the roof of the crocodile's mouth with a special spike on its head if the latter attempted to close its mouth. In another version, however, the crocodile was not so discourteous and moved its head as a signal that it intended to close its mouth.

As with many of the old animal stories, the reaction of modern scientists has been to pour scorn, then, somewhat begrudgingly, accept at least a basis of truth in them. Modern writers disagree as to the validity of the crocodile bird story but some report seeing birds that pick parasites off the crocodile's skin, entering their mouths as well. Sandpipers and Egyptian plovers have been seen taking leeches from the tongue.

These birds, apparently in great danger when performing these operations, are probably quite safe because animals such as crocodiles have very fixed patterns of behaviour. While basking, they are not interested in hunting, so even food in the mouth does not arouse them. This is also the explanation for small birds being able to nest within the nests of eagles with complete safety. That is, so long as the bird is on its nest its hunting instincts are inhibited.

class	**Aves**
order	**Charadriiformes**
family	**Glareolidae**
genera & species	**Cursorius cursor** *cream-coloured courser* **C. temminckii** *Temminck's courser* **C. coromandelicus** *Indian courser* **Peltohyas australis** *Australian dotterel* **Pluvianus aegyptus** *Egyptian plover* *others*

The double-banded courser, unlike its relatives, only lays one egg. Observers once saw a double-banded courser lay its egg at the height of the dry season in northern Tanzania—and both parents then took turns at standing over the egg (and later the chick) to keep it shadowed from the blazing sun. Other species will kick sand over their chicks to conceal them, and lure potential enemies away.

Arthur Christiansen

Courser *(family Glareolidae)*

◁ *Ranging from Africa to Australia, there are 9 species of courser—and 6 of them breed in Africa. The cream-coloured courser occasionally wanders north into Europe, and has sometimes been seen in Britain. Two species are reported in India, of which one —Jerdon's courser— is now probably extinct.*

Constance P Warner

△ *Restricted species: the baywinged cowbird, found in Argentina, Bolivia, Paraguay, Uruguay, and the coasts of Brazil.*

▷ *Widespread species: the glossy or shiny cowbird, ranging south from Venezuela as far as the central regions of Argentina.*

Cowbird

The three genera of cowbirds are related to grackles, troupials, and others. They are smallish birds, with glossy dark plumage. The shiny cowbird is 7 in. long with a conical, finch-like bill, and a glossy greenish-black and violet plumage. The screaming cowbird has a dull glossy plumage of blue-black with some green in the wings and tail. The common brown-headed cowbird of America, apart from the brown head, is greenish-black.

An American habitat

The various species of cowbirds are confined to America, most of them being found in the southern half of the continent. Some are fairly restricted. The baywinged cowbird, for example, is found in Argentina, Bolivia, Paraguay and Uruguay, and on the coasts of Brazil. The shiny cowbird, on the other hand, is widespread in South America from Venezuela and Colombia to the mid-region of Argentina. The brown-headed cowbird ranges across North America from the Pacific to Atlantic coasts. Its northern boundary runs from Nova Scotia, along the northern shores of the Great Lakes, up to the Great Slave Lake and down to Vancouver, and it ranges south to the borders of Mexico and Yucatan.

Cowbirds and cuckoos

Cowbirds could be called the cuckoos of the Americas because of the way they breed, although their common name is derived from their habit of following cattle to feed. They live in open country, spending the winter months in flocks and splitting into pairs that hold territories during the breeding season. Some species are sedentary; others, such as the shiny cowbird and brown-headed cowbird, migrate in spring and autumn.

A menace to growing crops

Cowbirds eat seeds and insects, the latter mostly during the summer when they are abundant. Many kinds of seeds are eaten and some cowbirds will feed on spilt grain around farmyards. In some places they are a considerable menace when they attack growing crops. This is especially so in the late summer when breeding is over. They descend on the ripening rice or corn fields in large flocks that are so dense that farmers kill 70 or 80 at a time with a double-barrelled shotgun blast.

At other times the cowbirds are beneficial, following the plough in search of grubs. This habit may be a development of their more usual one, of following cattle or other livestock to feed on the insects flushed from the grass by the large animals' hoofs. This is the reason for their name, and in some parts of North America they are called buffalo birds because before the buffalo (American bison) were killed off the cowbirds associated with them, walking behind the buffalo as they grazed or perching on their backs. An Indian legend describes cowbirds nesting in the wool between a buffalo's horns, and Ernest Thompson Seton tells of a cowbird that did not migrate one winter. Instead it made a nest in the wool on a buffalo's back in which to sleep.

The cuckoo's nesting habit

The parasitic habit of laying eggs in another bird's nest is not confined to the cuckoo. Several kinds of birds do this, including the cowbirds. Over 250 different species are parasitised by the brown-headed cowbird, although some are preferred to others. Most of its eggs are laid in the nests of its relatives, the orioles, but one study showed that up to 80% of song sparrow nests are victimised by various kinds of cowbirds. The female cowbird lays her eggs in the nest at the same time as the owner is laying hers, and before she has started to incubate them. By keeping a close watch, the cowbird notes

when the other bird leaves her nest, then she sneaks in and lays an egg in under a minute. Unlike the cuckoos, the baby cowbirds do not throw the other eggs out of the nest, but the adult cowbird will come back after laying her own egg and remove one or more in her bill.

Each cowbird lays four or five eggs, usually one in each of several nests, but if there is a shortage of nests several cowbirds will lay in one nest. As many as 37 shiny cowbird eggs have been found in the nest of one ovenbird.

Some birds reject the cowbird's eggs. Tyrant flycatchers build a new floor to the nest, covering the trespassing eggs. Others, such as catbirds and American robins, throw the eggs out, and some birds desert their nests altogether if they are parasitized. If, however, the cowbird egg is accepted it stands a very good chance of survival. Cowbird eggs hatch in a shorter time than the eggs of their host birds, so they have a good start in the competition for food that there always is between nestlings. Sometimes, this results in the death of the other nestlings, but not invariably so and two or three other nestlings, as well as the cowbird, may be reared. The young cowbird grows rapidly and leaves the nest in under two weeks, but it is still fed for another week.

Parental laziness

Not all cowbirds are parasites. The baywinged cowbird of South America rears its own offspring, both parents helping to feed the young. But even so there are some signs of the parental laziness of the true parasite. Very often the baywinged cowbird builds its own nest out of grass and feathers and most of the work is done by the male. However, if there are any abandoned nests of other species available, the cowbirds take them over, perhaps adding a few pieces of their own material. The next stage is represented by the screaming cowbird which ousts the rightful owner, who, surprisingly, is always the baywinged cowbird, while it is still in possession. From here one can see that a bird could merely take to laying its eggs in a nest rather than permanently displacing the owners. The shiny cowbird does this, and it has not completely lost the habit of nest building. During courtship it gathers nesting material and half-heartedly attempts to build a nest. At the end of this scale of increasing dependence on other birds is the brown-headed cowbird which no longer has any home of its own. It leaves its children on other people's doorsteps.

class	**Aves**
order	**Passeriformes**
family	**Icteridae**
genera & species	***Molothrus badius*** *baywinged cowbird* ***M. rufoaxillaris*** *screaming cowbird* ***M. bonariensis*** *shiny cowbird* ***M. ater*** *brown-headed cowbird* ***Tangavius armenti*** *Arment's cowbird*

Cowrie

The cowrie is a mollusc belonging to the same group as the sea snails (winkles and whelks) but with a shell which shows nothing of the usual spiral structure on the outside. The shell whorls laid down in the early life of a cowrie become enveloped during growth until only the final whorl is visible. On the underside of the mature shell is a long slit-like opening with its sides rolling inwards, like a scroll. The margins of the opening are grooved or toothed. The surface of the shell looks like highly polished porcelain, as it lacks the horny covering of many other shells. It is usually smooth, although in some of the smaller cowries it may be grooved. In life the shell is covered by the folds of that part of the mollusc's body known as the mantle. These meet at the mid-line of the upper surface, effectively protecting the shell from being scratched or otherwise damaged. The mantle is often ornamented with pointed or forked filaments.

Most cowries live on the coral shores of the tropics, in the Indian and Pacific

Oceans, north to Japan and south to New South Wales. They are also found in the Mediterranean and on both coasts of America. The largest are several inches long. In temperate seas there are fewer species and the shells are small and less ornate.

*The name is a corruption of **gowry,** from Hindi and Urdu. It seems to have come into the English language in the mid-17th century. The small European cowrie, also found on the coasts of the British Isles, has been called the nun in some localities and maiden stick-farthing or grotty buckie in others.*

Life between the tide-marks

Cowries are shallow-water molluscs sometimes living between tide-marks. Their mode of life is similar to that of other molluscs, their day alternating between resting periods and feeding sorties. When active the cowrie creeps over the bottom, its shell hidden by the mantle flaps on which are a number of small eyes. In many there is a pair of eyes in front, one near the base of each of the two sensory tentacles which are extended forward when the cowrie is moving. The tentacles are quickly withdrawn at the slightest disturbance.

Carnivorous sea snails

The more usual sea snails feed on seaweeds, rasping pieces from them with a file-like tongue or radula. Cowries are carnivorous although some also eat the smaller algal growths. The usual food is, however, small anemones, sponges, the eggs and egg-capsules of other sea snails, compound ascidians (sea squirts), coral polyps and the dead bodies of other molluscs. The mouth is at the end of a tube-like proboscis through which the radula is protruded.

A mothering mollusc

The breeding methods of the various species differ slightly in the way the eggs are laid. The European cowrie makes a small hole in the jelly of a mass of compound ascidians and in this deposits a vase-shaped capsule, about $\frac{1}{4}$ in. high, containing several hundred bright yellow eggs. One cowrie will deposit a number of such capsules over a short period of time. Fertilisation is internal and the sperms are stored, each batch of eggs being fertilised as it is laid. The nut-brown cowrie of the Pacific coast of the United States, $1\frac{1}{2}$ in. long, lays its eggs in July in rounded capsules, pointed at the apex, in batches of 100 forming a roughly circular plate nearly 2 in. across. Each capsule contains 800 eggs, and the plate formed by the tightly-packed capsules is guarded for 3

Colin G Butler

Anthony Bannister: NHPA

Hanging by its foot, a European cowrie displays its ribbed, porcelain-texture shell.

weeks by the cowrie which expands its foot into a circular sheet and allows this to 'hover' over the plate of capsules.

The larvae hatching within a capsule make their way out through an opening in the top of the capsule and are free-swimming for a while. Then each begins to grow a shell, descends to the sea-bed and grows into a young cowrie with at first a spiral shell. Gradually the spiral shell is overgrown by the last whorl after which growth ceases, whereas in other molluscs growth is continuous throughout life.

In cowries the central column, or columella, of the early spiral shell is dissolved and absorbed by the mollusc and the chalky material used to lay down the final shell. In any shell-forming marine animal the storage of calcium in the tissues prior to an addition to the shell must be considerable. Calcium is present in the sea in relatively very small quantities but marine animals are highly efficient in extracting it. Nevertheless, they cannot afford to waste any. Indeed, the material must be absorbed and re-used.

Cowries as cash

The common cowrie in the Indian Ocean is the money cowrie *Cypraea moneta*. Its shells have been used in trade from very early times until fairly recently in parts of

the Malay Archipelago, in the Maldive Islands and other areas fringing the Indian Ocean, to Africa. They have even been carried from the Indian Ocean, where they live, as far as Scandinavia and parts of North America, where they were used by the North American Indians. In West Africa cowries were a medium of exchange until a little over a hundred years ago, and the use of these shells as currency spread well inland into the heart of Africa, even to Timbuctoo. In the coastal areas of Africa the shells were threaded in strings of 40 or 100, 50 of the first and 20 of the second being worth about 3 half-crowns, or one American dollar. This is a considerable bulk of shells for so small an amount of cash yet it apparently paid people to import them, from all over the Indian Ocean area, into England, then re-export them to countries where they formed currency. In 1848, for example, 60 tons of money cowrie were imported into Liverpool, destined for re-export.

It matters not whether coin or cowrie forms the currency, the inherent weaknesses of men are still associated with it. In the coastal regions of West Africa, we are told, the people simply exchanged cowries in strings. Farther inland, for fear of being swindled, the people laboriously counted the shells one by one.

Cowries are undoubtedly attractive shells,

but this would hardly explain their widespread use. Part of the explanation is said to lie in the female appearance of the shell's aperture and the cowrie, once known as *Concha venerea*, was associated with the worship of Aphrodite which was inaugurated and centralized in Cyprus (hence the generic name *Cypraea*). It is therefore easy to understand its use as a charm to promote fertility and it is thence a short step to its use in ensuring rebirth after death. Perhaps the placing of cowries in the eye-sockets of mummies needs no such idea for its inspiration, since the underside of the shell is like a half-closed eye, but this practice may be related in turn to the supposed powers to repel the evil-eye and to bring luck and so to their use in games of chance. The study of these customs, often remarkably similar in different parts of the globe, can help in tracing the migrations and intercourse of early peoples.

phylum	**Mollusca**
class	**Gastropoda**
order	**Pectinibranchia**
family	**Cypraeidae**
genera & species	*Cypraea europaea, C. moneta Zonaria spadicea*

Coyote

*The coyote belongs with domestic dogs and wolves in the genus **Canis**. The name comes from the Mexican **coyotl** and can be pronounced with or without the 'e' silent. A coyote weighs 20—50 lb and measures about 4 ft from nose to tail-tip. The fur is tawny and the tail, bushy with a black tip, droops low behind the hind legs, instead of being carried horizontally as wolves do. Another difference from wolves is that coyotes are smaller, and they hunt smaller game than wolves.*

Coyotes used to live on plains and in woods of the western part of North America, being known as the brush wolf in forested regions and the prairie wolf in open lands. Within the last century their range has increased despite persecution and they are now found from north Alaska to Costa Rica. They have also spread eastwards to the Atlantic seaboard. At the turn of the century they had reached Michigan; they were seen in New York State in 1925 and in Massachusetts in 1957. The northward spread carried them to the southern shores of Hudson's Bay by 1961.

The prairie wolf's spread

In the face of man's persecution most carnivorous animals have been retreating. Their habitat has been destroyed and they are hunted mercilessly as vermin or as valuable fur bearers. The coyote is extending its range. There is no market for its fur but the coyote has long been shot on sight, or trapped and poisoned, because it has been regarded as an enemy of livestock and a competitor against man for game. Many thousands have been killed—125 000 a year according to one estimate—yet the coyotes flourish. Their powers of survival seem to lie in their proverbial wariness and their adaptability. They are difficult to trap unless a ruse is employed. One coyote avoided every trap set for it until the trapper buried an alarm clock near a trap and the coyote, overcome by curiosity, walked right into it.

The spread into the northeast United States is probably linked with widespread tree-felling and the decline and extinction of the timber wolf. This left a gap in the wildlife of the area which the adaptable coyote was able to fill. Even urban development has not deterred coyotes. They have moved into suburbs where, like the red fox in Britain, they can supplement their diet with gleanings from dustbins and other sources. There is a story of a Californian who wondered why his dog was not gaining weight despite being very well fed. He later discovered that a pair of coyotes were stealing its food. One lured the dog away while the other bolted the contents of the feeding bowl.

Give a dog a bad name . . .

Coyotes are persecuted because of their reputation as killers of livestock and deer. While sheep, goats and deer are occasionally killed, the reputation has probably been encouraged by the coyote's carrion-eating habits. A half-eaten carcase of a cow or sheep with coyote tracks around it leads to the assumption that coyotes killed it, and revenge is extracted without thought that the animal might have died for some other reason, such as thirst.

As proof that coyotes are not major threats to livestock, several thousand dead coyotes have been examined. Their stomachs contained mainly jack rabbits and cottontails, together with mice, voles and other small rodents. Poultry and livestock made up about $\frac{1}{8}$ of the sample. It is probable that, as with other animals with a varied diet, coyotes will eat whatever is most available. If rabbits are abundant, then poultry runs are left alone, but if a square meal in the form of a weak calf is found,

then it is not overlooked. Many other items are eaten; insects, birds, trout and crayfish have been found in coyote stomachs. Beavers, domestic cats, skunks and even grey foxes have been known to be attacked and eaten. Sometimes coyotes eat large amounts of vegetable matter, including prickly pears, grass and nuts. They are said to be very fond of water melons, taking only the ripe ones.

Coyotes hunt singly or in pairs, running down their prey with speeds of over 40 mph. Sometimes they chase deer in relays, one coyote taking over the pursuit as another becomes tired. Another habit is to sham dead, waiting for inquisitive, carrion-eating birds such as crows to land and examine the 'corpse', when it leaps up and grabs them.

Coyotes are model parents

Breeding begins when coyotes are a year old and they pair for life. They mate during January to March and the pups are born 63 days later. The den is usually made in a burrow abandoned by a woodchuck, skunk or fox, which is enlarged to form a tunnel up to 30 ft long and 1–2 ft in diameter, ending in a nesting chamber which is kept scrupulously clean. Nests are sometimes made on the surface—for

instance, in marshlands where tunnels would be flooded.

Up to 19 pups may be born in a litter, the average being around 10. They are born with their eyes shut and stay underground for over a month. The father stays with the family, bringing food first for the mother, then for the pups; this is regurgitated to them as a partly-digested mess. Later the family go out on communal hunting trips and the pups learn to hunt for themselves. Although hunters themselves, coyotes are not immune to being attacked by larger predators, and coyotes are known to have been killed by wolves, golden eagles and pumas.

The call of the West

Scientifically the coyote is *Canis latrans*, barking dog, so-called because apart from the domestic dog it is the only member of the dog family that habitually barks. Foxes, wolves and jackals only bark at specific times. The call of the coyote has become part of the background to the Wild West, necessary to produce 'atmosphere' for any night scene in a Western film. Coyotes can be heard all the year round, usually at dawn and dusk. In the evening coyotes sing in chorus. One starts with a series of

short barks, gradually increasing in volume until they merge into a long yell. Other coyotes join in and the chorus continues for a minute or two. After a pause, the chorus starts again.

Two or three coyotes may meet each night to sing and the eerie effect of the songs of several such groups ringing over the countryside on a still moonlight night is very impressive. Not surprisingly, there are numerous legends connected with the coyotes' song. The faraway sound is supposed to be made by the coyote barking into a badger hole to produce a hollow echo, while the quavering howl is said to be produced by the coyote making its chest vibrate by bouncing on rigid legs.

Many Indians claimed to understand the coyotes' language. The Comanches had their equivalent to Kipling's Mowgli, who was brought up by coyotes and later taught his tribe to understand them.

class	**Mammalia**
order	**Carnivora**
family	**Canidae**
genus & species	***Canis latrans***

Winter feast: coyotes clean an elk carcase while ravens wait for their turn.

Ed Park: Photo Res.

△ *Coyote pups. Up to 19 may be born in one litter, but the average is 10. After a month underground, the pups begin to sally out on communal hunting trips until they learn to fend for themselves.*

▽ *Suspicion: a swimming coyote approaches the bank. Hunters themselves, coyotes are known to have been attacked by larger predators.*

Des Bartlett: Photo Res.

Des Bartlett: Photo Res.

Coyote: the fast-loping prairie wolf

▷ *A coyote heads in to intercept a deer. When it comes to a straight chase, coyotes often find themselves outpaced by deer, and have been known to wear down their quarry by chasing in relays until it tires.*

▽ *A coyote in its classic pose as the spirit of the North American prairie—but within the last century they have spread across North America from Alaska to Costa Rica.*

▽▷ *A young coyote emerges from its lair. Coyotes live in scrupulously clean nesting chambers at the end of tunnels which can be up to 30 ft long.*

Joe Van Wormer: Photo Res.

Joe Van Wormer: Photo Res.

Coypu

The coypu is a large rodent that has been introduced to England where its presence has come to be regretted. It is a relative of the porcupines, but in appearance is rat-like, measuring over 3 ft from the large, square muzzle to the tip of its round, scaly tail. The ears are short and the small eyes set high in its large face give an air of stupid simplicity more profound than other rodents.

The coypu is adapted for an aquatic life, with webbed hind feet and long, coarse guard hairs effectively protecting the soft waterproof underfur. The underfur is the nutria of furriers, the name being an alternative to coypu and Spanish for otter. The finest underfur is on the underparts, so they are skinned by cutting along the back.

Reared for their fur

Coypus are natives of central and southern South America where they are widely distributed in swamps and along watercourses. During the 19th century they were extensively hunted for their fur and numbers dropped until laws were passed for their protection. Numbers rose again, then crashed as an epidemic struck. By this time, coypus, like other fur-bearing animals such as the chinchilla and mink, were being exported from their native homes and reared on farms. Like other fur-bearers, they escaped and went wild in their new homes. There are now wild populations of coypus in North America, England, several countries in Europe, and the USSR.

In England coypus were first found wild shortly after the farms were set up in the 1930s. Then before and during the Second World War they were released in large numbers as the farms closed down. The coypus colonised rivers and marshes, especially in the Norfolk Broads, and rapidly increased. At first there was no particular worry about them. Their burrows did not seriously undermine the banks and they were even considered beneficial because they cleared watercourses of the plants that choked them. The only complaints were heard when the coypus cut and trampled the reeds that were harvested for thatching. Later, as they increased in numbers, coypus began attacking crops and there were fears that their burrows, normally above the waterline, would cause extensive flooding when water levels were very high. Accordingly, a campaign to exterminate them was started in 1962. The coypus were then widespread in East Anglia, reaching into the counties of Northamptonshire, Lincolnshire and Cambridgeshire. The policy was to contain the spread, then drive them back. This has been successful, mainly because the hard winter of 1962−3 killed off most of the population. Now the breeding population is confined to the Norfolk Broads, with only stragglers being found elsewhere.

Coypus are rather solitary animals living among dense aquatic vegetation where

Philip Wayre: NHPA

△ *Coypus live among dense aquatic plants. Although they are most active at evening and night, they can sometimes be seen by day.*

▽ *Night feeding session; the coypu at right is eating a mare's tail weed. Coypus seem to prefer the more fibrous water weeds and grasses.*

John Markham

they make runs and build nests. Burrows are not always made and are not very extensive. Most activity takes place during the evening and night, but they are sometimes seen out on frosty days.

Coarse food is preferred

The parts of plants that coypus seem to prefer are not always the most succulent. They seem to like the tissues around the base of plants including the roots. Rushes, sedges, reed mace, Canadian water weed, water grasses and water parsnip are all listed as being in the coypus' diet and most of them are fibrous. Coypus became really unpopular when they moved away from the river banks and attacked fields of crops, notably sugar beet, which is grown in large quantities in East Anglia. Before the campaign against them had begun there were graphic reports of lines of coypus, easily visible in the moonlight, eating their way across sugar beet fields, the air filled with the noise of chewing. Other root crops and brassicas were also attacked and wheat pulled down for the grain.

As well as vegetation, coypus often eat freshwater molluscs, such as snails and mussels.

Babies suckled in the water

In England, coypus breed throughout the year, raising 2 litters of up to 9 babies, after a gestation of 100–130 days. In South America litters of 11 are known. The babies are well-developed at birth: their eyes are open, they have full coats of fur, within a few hours they can move around, and when a few days old they begin taking solid food. The mother's nipples are on the sides of her body so that the babies can feed while she lies on her stomach, and, more importantly, they are above the surface when she swims, so she can feed the babies without coming ashore.

Coypus are weaned when 2 months old and they may breed only a month later, before they are fully grown.

The coypu's enemies

In South America, jaguars and other large carnivores feed on coypus, but in England the adults are safe. Normally docile, they can defend themselves with their teeth. The young ones are preyed on by stoats, otters, rats, hawks and owls.

Greatest rat on earth

Fairground sideshows are better known for original ideas and style of presentation than for actual content, and the coypus presented the barkers with yet another fabulous creature that was worth a few pence to see. Before they became a pest, coypus were even more unfamiliar to the public than they are now, for it is doubtful whether many people connected nutria furs with the shaggy-haired coypu. So there was no difficulty in billing this rather ugly creature as a giant sewer rat. The idea of it lurking in untold numbers, separated from civilised society by only a manhole cover, must have added to the interest, and this was reinforced by paintings of coypus with bared teeth and yellow eyes resisting capture in subterranean tunnels. During the war its title was some-

Geoffrey Kinns AFA

△ *A swimming coypu enjoys a quick snack. Coypus are well-equipped for swimming, with webbed hind feet and a shaggy protective top coat of fur. The female's nipples are above the surface when she swims, so she can feed her young without coming ashore.*

Coypu *(Myocastor coypu)*

◁ *Like the chinchilla, the coypu is a native of South America which has been exported to North America and Europe for its fur. But the chinchilla has never approached the coypu's ability to thrive to the extent of becoming a pest—especially in England.*

times modified to 'giant rat caught in the blitz' but it is difficult to see why it should be caught, especially at a time when everyone was concerned with more important things. Whatever the source of the animals, they were at least more genuine than many a tattooed lady and two-headed monster.

class	**Mammalia**
order	**Rodentia**
family	**Capromyidae**
genus & species	*Myocastor coypu*

Crabeater seal

Of the five true seals living around the coasts of the Antarctic, the crabeater is the smallest. It is a slender, lithe animal with a small head, measuring at most 8 — 9 ft from snout to tail and weighing up to 500 lb. The females are usually slightly larger than the males.

The name white seal has been given to crabeaters on account of their creamy white fur, which is moulted in January (mid-summer in the southern hemisphere) to a greyish brown. During the year this fades back to white.

Life in the pack ice

Crabeaters are the most numerous seals in the Antarctic, if not in the world. Estimates of their numbers range from 2 — 5 million, accurate estimation being difficult because they live in the pack ice where man can reach them only by icebreaker or aeroplane. Counts of seals are regularly made from ships threading their way through the ice fields, and crabeaters are noticeably more common than other seals,

but the number of seals seen basking on the ice floes is not a true indication of their real numbers. It is impossible to know how many other seals are in the water. This number depends, at least in part, on the weather, for seals prefer to come out in calm, sunny conditions.

In summer the crabeaters move south as the pack ice breaks up, and they are found closer to the shore. When more detailed studies can be made it may be found that they have proper migrations from north to south. Some individuals wander north, reaching Australia, New Zealand and Uruguay.

Crabeaters can move over the ice at surprising speed. They throw themselves forwards by pushing at the packed snow and ice with hind and front flippers in a sort of undulating, caterpillar-like action. Speeds of 15 mph have been recorded.

They eat krill, not crab

Most seals feed on fish, and crabeaters are no exception, but their main food is the shrimp-like crustacean called krill, the same animal that forms the staple diet of penguins, whales and many Antarctic sea birds. So 'krilleater' would be a better name.

To catch krill in sufficient numbers to be efficient, crabeaters have a device to strain them from the water very much like the baleen plates that the blue whale, for instance, uses to to strain krill (see p. 384). In crabeater seals the teeth act as a strainer. Each tooth has five cusps, like battlements on a castle. The seal sucks in a mouthful of krill and water, then shuts its mouth so the teeth on upper and lower jaws fit closely together. It then forces water out through the gaps between the cusps, leaving the krill behind. The straining system is completed by bony growths at the back of the jaws that fill the gap behind the teeth that is present in other mammals. (This gap can be felt by feeling behind one's rear teeth with the tongue while the mouth is shut.)

The peculiar shape of the crabeater's teeth is probably derived from the sharp, cusped teeth of other seals, like the leopard seal, which are used to grip the slippery bodies of fish and squid.

Breeding at sea

Because crabeaters bear their pups in the remote fastnesses of the pack ice, little is known about their breeding habits. Females are thought to mate first when 2 years old,

A group of crabeaters lounges on an Antarctic floe. They are the most numerous seals in the Antarctic, if not the whole world.

bearing their single pups a year later, in October. Although crabeaters often gather on the ice in large numbers, pupping takes place in small groups. They prefer ice where the floes are not too closely packed together, but have been thrown into hummocks which provide shelter from the wind.

The newborn pups are about 4 ft long, 55 lb in weight and are covered in a soft, woolly coat. Information differs as to whether the pups are suckled for 2 or 4 weeks. The baby coat is presumably shed when the pup is weaned and it takes to the sea to fend for itself.

Crabeaters are believed to live for at least 29 years.

Mutilated by killer whales

Before anything else was known of the life of crabeaters, explorers in the Antarctic had noticed that they sometimes bore huge scars running the length of their bodies. It is surprising that the seals could survive such injuries until it is realised that only the blubber and surface muscles are cut open, so there is no serious damage. It was once thought these scars were the legacies of attack by killer whales but examination of a killer whale's mouth shows that its teeth could not fit the scars. The suggestion now is that the scars are from bites by leopard seals when the crabeaters are very young.

Crabeater mysteries

The survey base at Hope Bay is at the northern tip of the Antarctic Peninsula, and just to the south of it is the Crown Prince Gustav Channel that separates James Ross Island from the mainland. For most of the year the channel is frozen over and survey parties find it a convenient route for their sledging trips. In the winter of 1955 they were surprised to find vast concentrations of crabeater seals on the ice. Groups of several hundred, and one of a thousand, were counted in various parts of the channel, to make a total of 3 000 seals, ten times more than usual. More surprising was that 2 months later, in mid-October, most of these seals had died. In one large group only 3% survived. Samples of their internal organs were preserved and sent back to England where it was found that the seals had died from a disease. Some monstrous epidemic had spread through the population, creating the same sort of deathroll as myxomatosis among rabbits.

But the difference between the crabeater disease and myxomatosis is that the former has not spread through the whole population. This outbreak is an isolated instance and until more are recorded it must remain a mystery.

Another mystery is that of the skeletons and mummified bodies of crabeaters that were found 30 miles inland and 3 000 ft above sea level. For animals that are rarely found even hauled out onto beaches, this was a prodigious journey for apparently no reason. Then a few years ago a crabeater pup was found far inland. It had only recently died of starvation and bore the marks of a long journey over rocks. We can only presume that it got lost and went the wrong way as, presumably, the strays found on the shores of Australia and South America must have done.

class	**Mammalia**
order	**Pinnipedia**
family	**Phocidae**
genus & species	***Lobodon carcinophagus***

Crabeaters at a breathing hole in the pack ice, over which they can move at speeds of up to 15 mph.

Martin G White

Crab-eating fox

Also called the crab-eating dog, the crab-eating fox is a member of the dog family but is neither a true dog nor a true fox. This reflects a weakness in the English language, which contains names for only the three members of the dog family that have lived in the British Isles, the domesticated dog, the fox and the wolf. As a result, foreign names have been borrowed for the other members, such as coyote, or they have been given various names ending in dog, fox or wolf, depending on size or appearance.

In South America there are several members of the dog family so named, including the bush dog (p. 463) and the now extinct 'Antarctic wolf' of the Falkland Islands. The crab-eating fox is certainly fox-like with a sharp muzzle, pointed ears and bushy tail. The fur is short and of varying colour, ranging from pale grey to dark brown with yellowish brown or black in parts. The ears have a dark tip. The head and body are about 2 ft long with a tail of 1 ft.

Domesticated foxes

The crab-eating fox is the common fox of Colombia and Venezuela and is found south to Peru, southeastern Bolivia, northern Argentine and Uruguay, wherever there are tropical and subtropical woods. It is found in woodland, on mountains and plains and along the banks of rivers, inhabiting areas of scattered trees as well as denser woods. This is shown in its South American names: either wood fox or *zorro de monte*.

It has been said that the crab-eating fox hunts in parties of five or six, but this is probably based on observations of family groups. It is usually solitary or hunts in pairs at night, spending the day in the abandoned burrow of some other animal.

Crab-eating foxes are sometimes caught while young by South American Indians and mated with domestic dogs to produce hybrids that are apparently very useful for hunting small animals. It has been said that the Spaniards used a similar cross for hunting hutias, a coypu-like rodent, in the West Indies. This is unlikely, however, as there are no native foxes in the West Indies.

A misleading name

The main food of the crab-eating fox is not crabs but small mammals and birds which it hunts by scent in woodlands and runs down in open country. Insects, mostly grasshoppers, frogs and lizards, are also eaten. The crab-eating fox takes fruit as well, such as figs and berries, more often than is usually appreciated. When living near rivers the crab-eating fox catches freshwater crabs—hence its name—but it also eats molluscs and other animals living in the shallows. On the plains it catches small tortoises and also digs out their eggs.

Breeding

Very little has been published on the family life of the crab-eating fox. Litters of 1—5

Living paradox: although referred to as the crab-eating fox, it is neither a true dog nor a true fox, nor are crabs its main diet. A common fox in South America, it hunts small mammals and birds; it often eats insects, frogs, lizards, tortoises and their eggs, not to mention fruit. Freshwater crabs are only one of the items taken when the crab-eating fox hunts by river shallows, together with molluscs and other water creatures. It seems likely that it provides yet another example of an animal that has been given a premature name before all the facts were known—but a name which has stuck.

cubs have been born in zoos between March and August and 5 cubs, with their eyes still closed, were found in a field in September, suggesting that they are not always born in an underground den.

Not favoured by furriers

The fur is less valued than that of other South American 'dogs' and 'foxes' because of its shortness. In Buenos Aires it is marketed as 'Brazil fox' or 'provincial fox'.

Do they eat crabs?

The early naturalists are responsible for giving this fox its common English name, and at one time it was known scientifically as *Canis cancrivorus* (from Latin *cancer*—crab). They affirmed that crabs were the main item of diet and that small mammals and birds, now known to be the main food, were eaten only when crabs were not available. The fox was reputed to dive into shallow water for crabs and even recent publications show the crab-eating fox swimming down to pick a crab off the riverbed, yet authoritative scientific works make no mention of this habit. Considering the name of the fox, they would be unlikely to overlook any such observations, more especially as members of the dog family are not usually good at swimming and diving. Very little is known of the South American bush dog, for instance, yet it is known that it swims and dives well. What seems likely is that the first naturalists saw the crab-eating fox along the banks of rivers, which formed

the best, if not the only, routes through the unopened South American continent, and that they were then seen to be feeding on crabs. It would not be the first time that an animal had been given a name based on inadequate, or incorrect, knowledge.

class	**Mammalia**
order	**Carnivora**
family	**Canidae**
genus & species	*Cerdocyon thous*

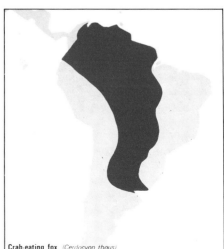

Crab-eating fox *(Cerdocyon thous)*

Crab plover

The crab plover is placed in a family on its own as it is distinct from other waders both in form and habits. Its internal anatomy is like that of true plovers.

An unusual wader, about 15 in. long, it has conspicuous black and white plumage. Most of the body is white but the flight feathers and the back are black, so the crab plover resembles an avocet. The legs are long and the toes are partially webbed. The tail is short and the black bill is fairly long, powerful and heron-like.

Crab plovers are found on shores and on reefs around the coasts of the Indian Ocean, from Natal, in South Africa, and Madagascar around to the Andaman Islands, in the eastern Indian Ocean, and including the Red Sea and the Persian Gulf. They are only visitors in the southern parts of their range, going there after breeding on the shores, mainly from Somalia to the Andaman Islands.

Noisy and fearless

Crab plovers are noisy birds and quite tame, unlike many other waders. Outside the breeding season they are found in flocks and have been seen perching on hippopotamuses as they lie in the water. A flock may consist of several hundred crab plovers which fly or stand in tight formations making a raucous din that can be heard a mile or more away. Colonel Meinertzhagen, who contributed much to our knowledge of birds in the Red Sea and Persian Gulf area, has described his difficulty in obtaining a pair of crab plovers for museum specimens. He had the greatest difficulty in shooting two birds without injuring many others. Eventually one shot killed four crab plovers, but instead of the flock flying away, it gathered around the dead birds while individual members tried to rescue their companions by pushing them along. They flew away only when Meinertzhagen was 10 yd away, showing a disregard for humans quite unlike other waders, which may flee as soon as anyone comes in sight.

Feeding on the strandline

Crab plovers feed along the shore seeking out marine animals as they become stranded and exposed by the ebbing tide. They are aptly named, for their main prey is crabs. These are caught in the bill and banged against the ground until unable to escape. Small crabs are then swallowed whole and large ones ripped apart and eaten piecemeal. Worms, crustaceans and fish spawn are also eaten, as are shellfish which are first battered to crack them open.

Nesting in holes

The breeding habits of crab plovers are unlike those of other waders, for they nest in burrows in sand dunes. It is during the breeding season that the crab plovers leave the shores and move a little way inland to banks and dunes protected from storms. Here the crab plovers make their burrows

The crab plover—long legs, black-and-white plumage, and a heavy, businesslike bill.

in small colonies, honeycombing the ground so it becomes difficult to walk across the colony without the ground caving in under one's feet.

The burrows are like those made by puffins and some of the petrels. The opening, which may be on level ground or in a sandy cliff or bank, leads downwards at an angle, then curves upwards and runs for 4–5 ft before ending in a nest cavity only a few inches beneath the surface. As the floor of the tunnel is beneath the level of the nest cavity there may be some protection against flooding during heavy rainstorms.

Within the nest cavity, on the bare ground, a single, large, goose-sized egg is laid, which is again unusual, for waders usually lay two to four eggs. The incubation period has not, apparently, been recorded, neither is it known whether both parents incubate. The chicks hatch with a coat of down, as do the chicks of other waders. They are also able to run shortly after hatching, but they stay in the nest cavity until fully-fledged, being fed by both parents on live crabs and other shore creatures.

A curious egg

The egg of the crab plover is worthy of attention for several reasons. For one thing it is white, whereas those of other waders, and gulls, which are also relatives of the crab plover, are noted for their speckled black or brown colours. But these birds nest in the open and their eggs must be very well camouflaged and difficult to find. On the other hand it is typical of birds nesting in tunnels or hollow trees to lay white eggs. In these situations camouflaged eggs are not necessary.

In proportion to its size the crab plover's egg is very large, a quarter of the adult's weight of 14 oz. To produce such an egg must throw considerable stress on the female, but in the long run perhaps not as much as the stress placed on birds that produce large numbers of small eggs. The crab plover is unusual, however, because, as a general rule, proportionately large eggs are produced in species where the young leave the nest shortly after hatching. In other words a large egg with plenty of food for the chick inside allows the chick to develop to an advanced stage before hatching. The crab plover is strange in that the chick is hatched in an advanced state but stays within the nest cavity.

class	**Aves**
order	**Charadriiformes**
family	**Dromadidae**
genus & species	*Dromas ardeola*

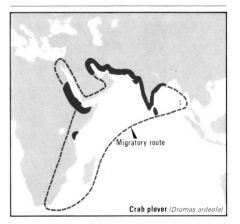

Migratory route

Crab plover *(Dromas ardeola)*

Crab spider

Crab spiders are so called because of the length and curvature of their legs and the way they scuttle rapidly sideways, like the true crabs of the sea shore. Crab spiders are all much alike wherever they are found. Many are found in flowers, the colours of which they often match to perfection. They make no web but lie in wait for their prey. They are represented in Britain by 39 species, many rare or of local distribution, and they range from very tiny to not much more than $\frac{1}{4}$ in. All but one of these belong to the family Thomisidae, there being a single representative of the family Sparassidae, the beautiful, green **Micrommata virescens** *which is comparatively large, the female being $\frac{1}{2}$ in. long, the male $\frac{1}{3}$ in.*

Beauty lies hidden

Crab spiders' colours or marks blend with their surroundings and this helps in capturing prey. Some spend most of their time in flowers, others lurk among leaf litter or low vegetation, and some lie along the stems or leaves of plants, head-downwards with the legs on each side held together in the same plane as the piece of foliage. Many combine effective camouflage with considerable beauty. *Thomisus onustus*, for example, is often a bright pink, blending perfectly with the flowers of the bell heath or certain orchids. Another, *Misumena vatia*, sometimes called the 'white death', occurs only in white or yellow plants, the white forms being found in flowers like the butterfly orchis, yellow varieties in mullein and gorse. If one of these spiders is transferred to a flower of a different colour, it quickly leaves it and seeks out another flower to match its own hue.

Danger in a flower

As the crab spider seizes its prey it pumps a poison into the victim's body along channels in its sharp-pointed jaws. This quickly affects the insect's nervous system or its blood, or both at once. The paralysed prey is then drained of its body fluids through the cuts made by the jaws. The husk is discarded. A wide variety of small insects and other invertebrates is taken.

Those crab spiders which lurk in flower heads often take insects like hover-flies, bees and butterflies which visit the flowers for nectar. Sometimes the prey is bitten in a non-fatal part, such as the abdomen, in which case the spider manipulates it until it is able to administer the *coup de grâce* in the head or thorax where the central nervous system can be more directly reached.

Captive courtship

A few days before the male undergoes his final moult he builds a small band of web on which to discharge a drop of seminal fluid. This he takes up into each of his two palps and then goes in search of a mate. There is little preliminary courtship, only tentative caressings with the legs which enable the two partners to recognise each other and which stimulate the female to

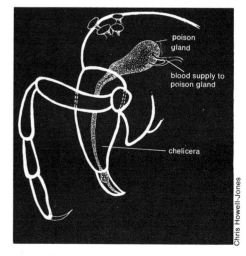

△ *Sudden death for a honey bee in the Transvaal veld. The spider has selected a flower in which its own colour will not be noticed by the victim until too late. Crab spiders kill by striking at the victim's head and thorax.*

▷ *The crab spider's hypodermic. The venom is held in the sac-like gland, which is covered with secretory cells. Muscle fibres encircle the gland; when they are contracted, venom is forced down the long duct running through the chelicera (fang).*

poison gland

blood supply to poison gland

chelicera

Anthony Bannister: NHPA

Chris Howell-Jones

692

△ *The face of an assassin: head-on view of a crab spider showing groups of eyes and pedipalps hiding the chelicerae or poison fangs.*
▽ *Female crab spider, with male. Like other spiders, mating is fraught with peril for the male crab spider, for the female will often seize and kill the male. In one species the male ties down the female until mating is completed and he can make good his escape.*

accept the male. Grasping the female by a leg the male inserts the sperm package in her genital aperture. If she has already mated she will not allow the male to approach but menaces him by raising her front legs and jerking her body. If he persists she may well seize and kill him. Mating may last for less than a minute or go on for several hours.

In one species *Xysticus cristatus* the male employs a device to prevent the female from seizing him. He binds her legs to the ground with threads of silk, after caressing her into accepting his initial advances. When mating is over the female is delayed just long enough in freeing herself from her bonds to allow the male to make good his escape.

Most crab spiders lay their eggs in early summer. The female makes a silken saucer into which to lay her eggs. This she then covers with another silken layer, forming a cocoon. It may be built between leaves lying on the ground or among foliage. Sometimes the female makes a silken tent within which she sits guarding the eggs. Many females eat nothing during the period of incubation, becoming extremely emaciated. Others capture prey as usual, though never straying far from their eggs. Young crab spiders are hatched as miniatures of their parents, though often differing considerably in colour. As in other spiders they grow by shedding their skins at regular intervals.

The cut-throat club

Spiders have many enemies. Small mammals, birds, reptiles and amphibians eat them, as do beetles, ants, and centipedes. Certain species of wasps and ichneumon flies lay their eggs in living crab spiders. Not least, considerable spider mortality is caused by different species of spider killing and eating one another. Indeed, it is likely that spiders indirectly play a major part in controlling their own numbers.

WS Bristowe, distinguished student of spiders, once estimated that the spider population of England and Wales alone was probably of the order of $2\frac{1}{5}$ billions (2 200 000 000 000) at any one moment—or some 40—50 thousand times the human population of Britain! If each spider eats only 100 insects a year, a conservative estimate, then the value of the service spiders render us in keeping insects down to a reasonable level is obvious. On a world scale it is incalculable.

Constance P Warner

△ *The crab spider's sharp-pointed jaws inject paralysing venom. It then drains the helpless victim of its body fluids.*

▽ *Crab spiders specialise in camouflage; this species is a perfectionist, even matching the flower's yellow-pointed stamens.*

KH Hyatt

phylum	**Arthropoda**
class	**Arachnida**
order	**Araneae**
family	**Sparassidae**
genus & species	*Micrommata virescens*
family	**Thomisidae**
genera & species	*Thomisus onustus* *Misumena vatia* others

Crake

Crakes are members of the rail family, and in North America they are known as rails. The Sora rail of America is occasionally found in Europe where it is known as the Carolina crake. The crakes are distinguished from other rails by a short conical bill.

The spotted crake is like a small corn-crake, with olive-brown upper parts streaked with white and a grey, white-speckled breast. The bill is yellow with a red base. Baillon's crake, the little crake and the Carolina crake are very like the spotted crake in plumage, but the first two are much smaller, being about starling size. The ruddy crake is intermediate in size with a dark brown back, reddish brown breast and a white chin.

Ubiquitous crakes

Like their near relative the corncrake, crakes are skulking birds living in thick cover and flying only short distances, except when on migration. Their capability for sustained flight is shown by the Carolina crake's trans-Atlantic flights; at least half-a-dozen have been recorded in the British Isles. The spotted crake has made trips in the opposite direction, turning up in Greenland and the West Indies.

Crakes have a world-wide distribution and are found in Madagascar, Australia, the Philippines and many other Pacific islands as well as on the main landmasses. The spotted, little and Baillon's crakes are found in Europe and Asia, and Baillon's crake is also found in southern Africa, Australia and New Zealand – an unusual discontinuous distribution with isolated populations in different parts of the world. The Carolina crake breeds in Canada and the United States, migrating south as far as Peru in winter and occasionally reaching Britain.

Crakes are now but rarely seen in Britain. The spotted crake used to breed regularly but in the 19th century extensive drainage works destroyed its breeding grounds. Now the occasional pair breeds in England, perhaps one a year on average. Baillon's crake occasionally bred in East Anglia during the 19th century. With the little crake, Baillon's crake is now a rare visitor to Britain.

Among the rail family there is a gradation of habitat. The corncrake (p. 668) prefers grassland and the coots (p. 654) require open sheets of water where they can freely dive. The crakes prefer intermediate conditions, among the marshy banks of rivers and lakes and in dense reed beds where there is a sodden mat of vegetation. The Carolina crake fills the same habitat in North America as the spotted crake in Europe, which keeps to the drier borders of swamps. Baillon's crake and the little crake prefer the flooded areas in the middle of the swamps, and the little crake in particular frequents marshes with open pools.

Swamp feeding

Crakes feed on the animals and plants they can find living at the surface of the swamp

Arthur Christiansen

Crakes are skulking birds, living in thick cover and never flying far unless on migration. They will usually lay 6–12 eggs, and the male and the female brood them in turn for 3 weeks.

water or in the mud and decaying plants between the pools. Their main food is water snails and insects such as water beetles, mayflies and mosquitoes, as well as their larvae. Water plants and grass are also eaten. In North America, the Carolina crake eats mainly seeds during the autumn, including those of wild rice.

Father looks after firstborn

The nests are built in swamps and marshes, either on tussocks of grass or small islands, but the Carolina crake and Baillon's crake sometimes build basket-like nests in clumps of sedge or other marsh plants, a foot or more above the surface of the water. The stems of the plants around the nests are interwoven to form a canopy hiding them from possible enemies. The nest itself is made of dead rushes and grasses and is lined with finer vegetation. The Carolina crake sometimes makes a runway of nesting material, leading up to the nest.

Crakes generally lay 6–12 eggs, the spotted crake being known to lay up to 15. Male and female brood them in turn for up to 3 weeks. As incubation starts before all the eggs are laid the chicks emerge at intervals over a period of several days. They can leave the nest shortly after hatching and the male cares for them while his mate incubates the younger eggs. Then both parents guard the chicks, feeding them until they are a week old. Sometimes the chicks split into two parties, each under the charge of one parent.

Which crake is which?

Crakes are undistinguished-looking secretive birds difficult to identify at the best of times, but their preference for living in marshes with thick vegetation, water and mud, not to mention swarms of mosquitoes, makes them very difficult to observe. Probably no other group of birds in Europe is so badly known. The description of their habits given above is only a general outline as the habits of no one species is well known.

The difficulty of identification and study is best illustrated by the story of a very competent ornithologist who embarked on a study of Baillon's crakes, but years later the birds he had watched were identified from his photographs as young little crakes. Since then Baillon's crakes have been identified in various parts of Europe by comparing their calls with a recording made in 1948. But in 1968 a bird making a call similar to this recording was trapped and found to be a female little crake.

class	**Aves**		
order	**Gruiformes**		
family	**Rallidae**		
genus & species	*Porzana porzana* spotted crake		
	P. carolina Carolina crake		
	P. parva little crake		
	P. pusilla Baillon's crake, others		

One of the most impressive cranes of all: the crowned crane, with its Roman-helmet crest, gives a good idea of how head and neck coloration can often be used to pick out the different crane species.

Crane

An elegant, long-legged, long-necked heron-like bird, the largest crane stands 5 ft high, with a wingspan of 7½ ft. There are 14 kinds of these impressive birds, most of them now rare. As they are very wary, disturbance of the cranes' habitat has caused their decline as much as hunting, but it seems that within historical times some species were never numerous.

Species are often distinguished by the patches of colour around head and neck. The common crane has a red crown with black and white on head and neck. The whooping, sandhill and sarus cranes and the brolga have red patches on the head. The crowned crane is often said to be the most striking. It has white ovals behind the eyes, a red wattle and a plume of orange-brown feathers, like the crest on a Roman helmet. Yet few birds can be more impressive than the Manchurian crane, with its starkly contrasting black and white plumage. The head and neck are black except for a white patch on the crown reaching to the eyes. The body is pure white except for the black secondaries, which form a black rear border to the wings when spread.

An unusual feature of cranes' internal anatomy is the windpipe, which may be 5 ft long, half of which is coiled within the breastbone. The enormous length of the windpipe gives the cranes their loud trombone-like calls, which carry for a mile or more.

A declining family

In many parts of the world, cranes' numbers are becoming reduced. They breed in lonely marshlands and swamps, which are becoming rarer. Shooting for sport or because the cranes damage crops has also taken a toll. The two cranes most in danger are the Manchurian crane and the whooping crane. The Manchurian crane survives in small numbers on the mainland of Siberia and in a secluded swamp on the island of Hokkaido in north Japan. The whooping crane is in a desperate plight. There were probably no more than 1 500 when Europeans arrived in America, now there are just over 70, all in one flock, and the population once went down to 22. A single disaster could annihilate them, as in 1939 when another whole flock was wiped out by a flood. Whooping cranes are particularly vulnerable, because each year they migrate from their breeding grounds in the Wood Buffalo National Park in Alberta, Canada, to a winter home on the shoreline of Texas. During this migration they have to run the gauntlet of hunters, power cables across their flight paths and other hazards, and it seems that their rate of reproduction can barely keep pace with deaths. The sandhill crane of North America is in a much better position and in places is increasing.

Apart from the sandhill and whooping cranes of North America, cranes belong to the Old World, but are not found in Madagascar, southeast Asia, New Zealand and Polynesia. The common crane lives in Europe and Asia, mainly in northern areas. In mediaeval times it was quite common in the British Isles, where it bred up to about 1600, but now only occasional visitors are seen. Yet in one week in October 1963 several hundred cranes were seen in south-ern England, and one flock of about 100 was seen near Midhurst in Sussex. These cranes were most likely to have been driven across the North Sea by bad weather.

Most cranes live in flocks and are migratory, moving from summer to winter quarters like the whooping crane described above. A migrating flock is a beautiful sight as the birds fly in V, or echelon, formation with slow, measured beats, and necks outstretched. During migration they fly at great heights, apparently up to 2 miles.

Feeding

Cranes eat mainly vegetation, including leaves, roots and fruit. Sometimes they attack crops and are persecuted for this. Overall, they probably help farmers, by eating harmful insects, thrusting their long bills into the soil to take wireworms and other larvae. Cranes also eat frogs, reptiles, small birds and mammals.

The dancing cranes

Throughout the year, but particularly in the breeding season, cranes indulge in a spectacular ritual dance. They walk around each other with quick, stiff-legged steps and wings half spread, occasionally bowing and stretching. The tempo of the dance increases, and they leap into the air, flying up 15 or more feet and drifting down in a slow-motion ballet. This dance is not confined to pairs of cranes, for sometimes whole flocks including juveniles will join together to dance — apparently from sheer high spirits. During the dance some of the cranes pick sticks or leaves with their bills, throw them into the air, and stab at them as they fall.

Cranes make their nests on the ground, piling up a heap of vegetation usually on open, marshy ground, sometimes in a few

inches of standing water. On dry ground the nest may be little more than a patch of flattened vegetation. The usual clutch is 2 eggs, the second being laid 2 days after the first, and because incubation starts immediately the first egg is laid it hatches 2 days before the second. The chick can run almost at once and, in the care of the male, leaves the nest, while the female continues to incubate the second egg. Later, when both chicks have left the nest, each may be taken care of by one parent. Their legs grow very rapidly and in one month are full grown while the wings have hardly developed. They do not fly until 9 or 10 weeks.

In Japan cranes are symbols of longevity and in folklore are reputed to live for 1 000 years. Even in real life they are known to live for at least 50 years.

The Tanchō of Hokkaido

The dance of the cranes must be one of the most spectacular performances in the bird world. Other birds have a more beautiful and elaborate plumage to set off their displays, but the cranes' size, combined with the grace and energy of their dances, makes them outstanding. Especially spectacular is the dance of a flock. The brolga of Australia, also known as the 'native companion', dances in troops lined up in rows of 20–30. The dance of the brolga is the basis for some of the dances at aboriginal corroborees, and there are crane dances in other parts of the world, where the cranes symbolise the returning spring. The aboriginal Ainu tribesmen of Japan have a dance commemorating the Tanchō or Manchurian crane.

The Manchurian crane often appears in Japanese art and literature and for hundreds of years it was protected by the Jap-

anese veneration of it as a symbol of eternal life. Only the emperor could hunt it, with goshawks, which were awarded a purple hood if they were successful in killing such a magnificent bird. The Buddhist ban on the taking of life also protected the cranes until Buddhism was ousted. Indiscriminate slaughter immediately took place, and the Manchurian cranes were exterminated in Japan except in the Kushiro swamp in Hokkaido. This swamp was inaccessible except when its waters froze, and its population of cranes did not migrate to areas where they would be more vulnerable. Nevertheless, numbers dropped to 20 in 1924, but strict preservation has allowed them to recover, and they now number about 200. In the winter they come out of the marsh and visit neighbouring farms, where the farmers feed them in return for the pleasure of seeing the cranes dance in the snow.

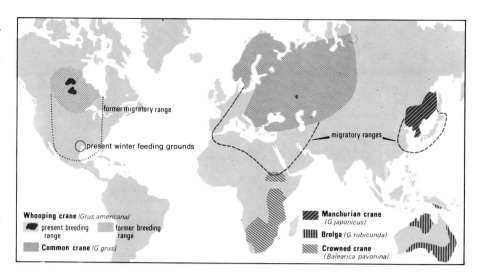

Whooping crane (Grus americana)
■ present breeding range
former breeding range
Common crane (G.grus)
former migratory range
present winter feeding grounds
migratory ranges
Manchurian crane (G.japonicus)
Brolga (G.rubicunda)
Crowned crane (Balearica pavonina)

class	**Aves**
order	**Gruiformes**
family	**Gruidae**
genera & species	***Grus grus*** common crane ***G. americana*** whooping crane ***G. japonensis*** Manchurian crane ***G. rubicunda*** brolga ***Balearica pavonina*** crowned crane others

Overleaf: Sandhill cranes. The long, loose 'bustle', formed by the secondary wing feathers hanging over the tail, is a characteristic feature.

Below left: Sandhill cranes show off their wing action in flight. The North American sandhills are holding their own and are on the increase in places.

Below right: The colourful, high-spirited dance of a group of crowned cranes.

Joe Van Wormer: Photo Res

Simon Trevor: Photo Res

Crayfish

The crayfish is a freshwater crustacean. It looks like a small lobster, 4 in. or more long, and coloured sandy yellow, green or dark brown. The head and thorax are covered with a single shell, or carapace, which ends in front in a sharp-pointed rostrum. Its eyes are compound and stalked. On its head is a pair of small antennules which are richly supplied with sense-organs, and a pair of long antennae, which are organs of touch. These have excretory organs at the base. The crayfish has a pair of strong jaws and two pairs of smaller accessory jaws, the maxillae. The second pair of maxillae drives water over 20 pairs of feathery gills on the bases of the thoracic limbs.

Preparing to carve: a freshwater crayfish about to feed off a male stickleback.

Jane Burton: Photo Res

On the thorax there are three pairs of appendages, which are used to pass food to the jaws, a pair of stout pincers and four pairs of legs, which the crayfish uses to walk forward. The abdomen is divided into segments and has five pairs of limbs on its underside. The first pair are grooved in the males and are used to introduce sperm onto the female. The other four are swimmerets. The crayfish can swim speedily backwards with forward flicks of its abdomen, which ends in a fan-shaped tail. It does this to escape.

Crayfish in cooler waters

The two families of crayfish are confined almost entirely to temperate regions: the Parastacidae in the northern hemisphere, the Astacidae in the southern hemisphere. There are no crayfish in Africa, but they are present in Madagascar. There is none in the greater part of Asia, but they are found in Korea and the northern islands of Japan. The largest crayfish *Astacopsis franklini* lives in Tasmania and may weigh up to 9 lb. Another large crayfish related to it is sold as Murray River Lobster in southeastern Australia. One of the Tasmanian crayfish, known as a land crab, habitually leaves the water and burrows in damp earth in forests. In the Mammoth Cave in Kentucky, in the United States, there are several crayfish living in the underground waters. They are colourless and blind; the eyes are gone, leaving only the stalks.

Naturalized aliens

Only one crayfish *Potamobius pallipes* is native to Britain. It is known as the white claw. A larger European crayfish *Astacus astacus*, reared on farms especially in France, has been introduced into the Thames, and is known as the red claw. An American species, introduced into Germany, has become established there. The three species have similar habits. They live in rivers and lakes, especially those with hard water which contains the lime needed for their shell. They feed mainly at night, resting by day in burrows in the mud or under stones, but can sometimes be seen moving about by day.

They eat smaller aquatic animals such as insect larvae, snails, worms and tadpoles, and a small amount of plant food. In the Mississippi Valley they graze on rice during the night. This infuriates the local farmers who regard them as pests.

Unusual breeding habits

Crayfish mate in the autumn. The male turns the female over and sheds milt through the first pair of abdominal appendages onto her abdomen, where it sticks. The female then goes into a burrow to lay her hundred or so eggs. These become attached to bristles on her swimmerets where they are fertilised by contact with the milt. The eggs hatch the following spring. Unusual for a crustacean there is no larval stage. The newly-hatched crayfish are transparent, and tiny replicas of the adults. They remain attached for some time to the female's swimmerets, which they grasp with their claws.

Life and death in crayfish

In many parts of the world, crayfish are considered a delicacy. Sometimes they are eaten raw although this can prove to be hazardous, because crayfish carry a fluke larva. If this is swallowed with a crayfish it will migrate through the wall of the gut to the lungs, where it matures to the adult parasite. In time the adult lays eggs which are ejected with the sputum. From the eggs hatch first stage larvae which infest snails. The cycle of parasitic infection is completed if a snail is eaten by a crayfish.

One interesting aspect of the life of a crayfish is that it grows by periodic moults. This is common knowledge and is often stated in books on natural history. Most crustaceans and insects grow like this. But although it is always stated simply, the process itself is complex. In crayfish it takes place in four stages. First the calcium salts, the chalky matter in the old shell, are taken back into the blood, ready to be laid down again in the new shell being formed beneath the old one. Then the old shell, or such as remains of it, now merely a tough cuticle, is shed and the body takes up water and swells. Then the calcium salts are laid down in the new cuticle and this takes time to harden.

The moult of a crayfish takes 6 hours. During this time the crayfish fasts and stays in hiding. It is a very dangerous period for it; not only is it vulnerable especially to enemies, but it is also in danger from the many attendant difficulties of the process itself. It has only recently been realized, in fact, that many crayfish die during this complicated moulting process.

phylum	**Arthropoda**	
class	**Crustacea**	
order	**Decapoda**	
families	**Parastacidae**	
	Astacidae	
genera & species	*Astacus astacus*	
	Potamobius pallipes	
	others	

△ *Male and female freshwater crayfish. Notice the egg clusters on the female (right), attached to bristles on her swimmerets. Crayfish mate in the autumn, and the eggs hatch in the following spring. Unlike most other crustaceans there is no larval stage: the young are tiny replicas of the adults.*

▽ *Transparent, fragile crayfish babies cling to the swimmerets of their mother. Crayfish grow by periodic moults, each lasting 6 hours.*

Creeper

The treecreepers are among several groups of birds called creepers, including the Australian treecreepers, the wallcreeper that is related to the nuthatch, and various members of the antbird, babbler and ovenbird families. Treecreepers, or simply creepers, as they are known in North America, a term to be preferred because it is more embracing, are sparrow-sized birds with brown, streaked plumage on the back and light underparts. They have slender, pointed bills and long curved claws. The tail looks tattered, as it is made up of stiff pointed feathers.

The common treecreeper ranges from the British Isles to Japan, and in North America, where it is known as the browncreeper, from Alaska to Nicaragua.

John Markham

Farther south it is replaced by the very similar woodcreepers. The short-toed treecreeper is also found in much of Europe, except the British Isles and Scandinavia, and spreads into Turkey and North Africa. Where the two species overlap, the short-toed treecreeper stays mainly in deciduous, broad-leaved woodland, while the common treecreeper lives in conifer forests. It has been suggested that the short-toed treecreeper does not live in the British Isles because it followed the spread of the broad-leaved trees as they moved north through Europe after the Ice Age. Before the short-toed treecreeper reached the British Isles, the common treecreeper had already arrived

in the wake of the conifers. The Straits of Dover then opened up, and the common treecreeper adapted itself to broad-leaved trees, as there was no competition from the short-toed treecreeper. The remaining three creepers live in the Himalayan region.

Creepers live on tree trunks

Creepers are woodland birds. They are not strong fliers, and are usually seen flitting from one tree to another or hopping jerkily up a tree trunk, peering from side to side in search of food, in the same way as nuthatches. The two are readily distinguishable by their plumage, and the creepers nearly always hop up the trunk, and when they descend go down backwards, rather than headfirst like a nuthatch. Creepers also use their stiff tail as a support, pressing it against the trunk, like a woodpecker.

At night, creepers roost in crevices in bark, under eaves, in ivy or in holes in dead or soft-barked trees, where they fluff out their feathers to keep warm. Sometimes groups of about 15 at a time will huddle together in a fluffy ball on cold nights, but at other times they show strict ownership, and a creeper will attack others that it finds in its roost.

Food found in bark

As a creeper climbs up a tree or along a branch it searches for insects, spiders and woodlice, together with their eggs and larvae, which it pulls out of crevices with its finely pointed bill. Seeds are very occasionally eaten. The bark of the tree is searched systematically; the creeper starts at the base and works spirally upwards. If it finds a particularly rewarding section it flutters down and goes over it again. When

one tree has been searched, the creeper flies to the base of the next.

Spiral courtship chase

Creepers' songs are very high-pitched thin trills, and so are as relatively inaudible to our ears as the birds are inconspicuous to our eyes. During courtship the male chases the female in spirals around tree trunks, or flies in spirals around the trunk where she is perching.

The nest of the common treecreeper, that is the North American browncreeper, is made in the same places as the roosts. It is an untidy mass of grass, moss and leaves, with a cup-shaped depression at the centre lined with feathers and bark.

The 4—7 eggs, usually 5, are incubated by the female alone, at least in North America. It seems that in Europe the male sometimes helps in incubation, although he does not have the featherless brood patch on his breast. Incubation lasts 15 days and the chicks spend a further 15 in the nest, being fed by both parents.

Creepers' roosts

In the 19th century there was a fashion in the British Isles for planting exotic trees and shrubs, with the result that Wellingtonias, monkey-puzzle trees and rhododendrons are now quite common in many parts of the country. In Scotland, in 1905, and in England a few years later, treecreepers were found to be making roosts in Wellingtonias by digging holes in the trunks about $2\frac{1}{2}$ in. diameter and 2 in. deep. Wellingtonia bark is soft and spongy. It is possible to punch it with all one's might and not hurt the knuckles, and creepers are able to peck holes easily.

The habit of making roosting holes in Wellingtonias spread rapidly through the country from 1930 onwards, and it is likely that this happened for two reasons. Creepers will dig holes in the soft wood of dead trees, and in California the browncreepers make holes in the native Wellingtonias and incense cedars. They prefer older trees with rough bark and it was during the early part of this century that the Wellingtonias planted in the British Isles were becoming rough. At the same time farmers and foresters no longer tolerated dead trees, so depriving treecreepers of their original roosting sites.

It is not difficult to see a creeper in its roosting hole if one knows where to find the hole. If this is being currently used there will be an accumulation of droppings on the bark under it. The creeper retires to rest at dusk, fitting neatly into the hole with tail hanging out, feathers fluffed and beak buried in its shoulder feathers. Once it has gone to sleep, it is quite easily seen with the aid of a torch.

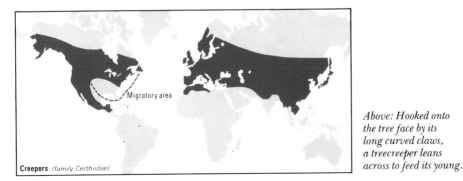

Creepers (family Certhiidae)

Above: Hooked onto the tree face by its long curved claws, a treecreeper leans across to feed its young.

class	**Aves**
order	**Passeriformes**
family	**Certhiidae**
genus & species	***Certhia familiaris*** *treecreeper or browncreeper* ***C. brachydactyla*** *short-toed treecreeper others*

Crested lark

The crested lark is a little smaller than a skylark, measuring 6¾ in. from head to tail. Several larks have crests, but these are not as conspicuous as those of the crested lark or the very similar thekla lark. Some ornithologists have placed these two larks in the same species, but it is now generally accepted that they are sufficiently distinct to be kept apart. It is very difficult to tell them apart in the field however. The thekla lark is smaller with shorter and narrower wings and it has a distinctly shorter and less pointed bill than the crested lark. The crest on the latter is reported to be more of a spike of feathers while that of the thekla lark consists of a complete fan. The two birds also have different songs.

Peter Johnson

The crested lark is only rarely found in the British Isles, when it comes over from the Continent. Its breeding range extends from the Atlantic coasts of France and Spain to Korea and covers northern India, Arabia, and North Africa, around the fringes of the Sahara, down the Red Sea coast to Ethiopia and Somalia. In historical times it spread up through Europe from the Mediterranean and between 1850 and 1900 it colonised parts of Scandinavia. It is now found in Denmark and nearby parts of Norway and Sweden. The thekla lark is found in Spain, North Africa (from Mauretania to Egypt) and in Ethiopia and Somalia. Where their ranges overlap the two larks generally breed in different habitats.

Bird of desert fringes

The crested lark usually lives on flat, rather barren, steppe country and the fringes of deserts where there are patches of sandy soil with coarse grass and low, thorny bushes. It is also common along roadsides, in gardens, and on waste land in towns. As the steppes of central Europe became cultivated it spread through the continents as other suitable habitats were formed along roads and railways that were being built.

Feeding

The crested lark lives mainly on grain, from oats and wheat and the seeds of grasses and weeds. During the winter it is not above picking the undigested grains out of horse droppings. In the breeding season, when it has a family of hungry chicks to feed, it catches beetles, grasshoppers and larvae.

Chicks sheltered from the sun

The song of the crested lark, a liquid whistle of three or four syllables, is like that of a skylark but is not so loud or continuous. Like the skylark, the crested lark sings high in the air, from as much as 100–200 ft up. It does not sing, however, while ascending or descending, so it is not so conspicuous as the skylark which rises slowly, singing all the time. The crested lark also sings while perched on houses, trees or telephone wires.

The nest is built by both sexes from grass stems which are woven into a cup and lined with rootlets or hair. The nests are under low bushes or in thick grass, but sometimes on roofs of sheds or houses. Usually they are sheltered from the glare of the midday sun and sometimes a dome is woven over the nest cup.

In Europe, 4 or 5 eggs are laid; in Africa and Asia Minor 5 or 6.

The female incubates the eggs

Incubation is by the female alone. In hot weather she does not sit on the eggs, but stands over them, sheltering them from the sun's heat. After the chicks have emerged, the female lark eats the eggshells or drops them 1 or 2 ft from the nest. The eggs hatch in 11–12 days and the chicks stay in the nest for a week or more, but they do not fly for at least another week.

Camouflaged larks

With the exception of the male black lark, members of the lark family have a brown plumage, streaked with grey or buff. The underparts are lighter and more uniform. When perched or feeding on the ground, or sitting on the nest, they are very hard to see. Most animals are inconspicuous when motionless, whatever their colour, but the larks, living in sparsely-vegetated margins of deserts, blend in particularly well with their background. Comparison of their

plumage with samples of the sandy soil on which they live has shown that the plumage tends to match the different soils. The matching shades enable the larks to merge against their background. This protects them from being spotted by enemies.

Crested and thekla larks that live in semi-desert areas match their surroundings particularly well. In one test 25 larks out of 33 were found to match the colour of the soil where they were living. This figure improved to 20 out of 22 when comparisons were made in the breeding season only. This suggests that the larks are especially adapted to suit the background colour of their breeding habitat, which would obviously have the most survival value. In Europe, however, the match is not so good; only 8 larks out of 14. matched the soil. This is probably because the vegetation is thicker than in North Africa and the larks' nests are not surrounded by bare soil.

Camouflage like this is not confined to the

Arthur Christiansen

Left: Feeding time for a crested lark family. Larks will normally nest on the ground, weaving grass stalks into a cup for the eggs, but they will sometimes nest on the roof of a shed or house. Crested larks lay 4 or 5 eggs in Europe, 5 or 6 in Africa and Asia Minor.
Above: Winter and rough weather: a crested lark dourly faces winter conditions by fluffing up its feathers to trap air for warmth. Although the wings of the crested lark are shorter than those of the skylark, the crested lark's wing area is considerably larger.

crested and thekla larks. Over their range, from North Africa eastwards, the plumage of sand larks also closely matches the various soil colours. In Arabia, for instance, where there are patches of black lava in the pale sand, there are two races of desert lark. The dark race lives on the lava and the light race on the sand. No amount of chasing will make them run on to ground of the wrong colour.

class	**Aves**
order	**Passeriformes**
family	**Alaudidae**
genus & species	***Galerida cristata*** *crested lark* ***G. thekla*** *thekla lark*

Crested porcupine

The porcupines of the Old World do not climb. Porcupines of the New World spend much time in trees. For this reason, and because of other differences, New World porcupines are placed in a separate family, which will be dealt with under tree porcupine.

One of the largest of the rodents, the crested porcupine is up to 28 in. long exclusive of its 5in. tail, and it may weigh up to 60 lb. It is brownish-black with a whitish band around the neck, and is heavily built with short stout legs. The body is covered with two kinds of quills; one set is short and stout, the other long and slender, and both are banded black and white. The long quills may be over 1 ft long and ¼ in. diameter. On the head and neck is a crest of long white bristles with brown bases. The quills on the rump are black, those on the tail are white.

The crested porcupine ranges across North Africa, from Morocco to the Sudan and southern Egypt, and is also found south of the Sahara from Senegal to tropical eastern Africa. It also occurs in Sicily and Italy, where it was probably introduced, and has recently been introduced into Albania and southern Yugoslavia. It is one of 8 species of Hystrix, all similar, distributed from South Africa through southern Asia to Indonesia. There are 7 more related species, 2 similar to Hystrix, 4 species of brush-tailed porcupines in Africa, and 1 long-tailed porcupine in Borneo and Sumatra.

Vegetarians that gnaw bones

Despite their strange spiny appearance porcupines are rodents and their quills are merely modified hairs. As with all rodents they have a pair of stout chisel-like incisor teeth in both upper and lower jaws. They grow continuously at the roots and need constant use, not only to keep them sharp but also to wear them down at the crowns to prevent them growing too long. This partly accounts for the porcupine habit of gnawing bones. Doubtless they also benefit from the lime and phosphorus salts in the bone.

Porcupines live singly or at most in pairs. They live chiefly on rocky hills with good undergrowth and spend the day in holes in the ground or among rocks, coming out at night to feed on roots, bulbs, bark and fallen fruits. Near cultivated land they can become a pest to crops.

Born with soft quills

Breeding takes place early in the year and, after a gestation of 63−112 days, 2−3 babies are born fully developed in a nest of leaves, grass and roots. Their eyes are open at birth and the quills are soft and flexible, but harden within the next 10 days. The young are at first striped black and white. In captivity porcupines have lived up to 20 years or slightly more.

Dreaded pincushion

It is doubtful whether porcupines suffer seriously from enemies. Only the larger carnivores such as leopards and hunting dogs can successfully attack them, and even these do so usually when very hungry and probably desperate. They can more easily take the young, and experienced predators learn to flip a porcupine over and attack the soft underbelly. There are stories from Africa of lions, and more particularly elderly lionesses with cubs to feed, who have tried conclusions with porcupines as age or damaged teeth prevented their killing more rapidly moving prey. Even so, they have paid for it with quills painfully embedded in the mouth or paws.

A porcupine's defence is to raise and spread its quills, rattle them to give warning of attack and then to rush backwards at the enemy. The quills are only loosely embedded in the skin so they easily become detached and embedded in the enemy's flesh. After that, because of their barbed points, any movement causes them to work their way in deeper and deeper, and they have been known to end up in the heart or some other vital organ.

The main danger to porcupines is that man eats their flesh. Africans, especially, catch porcupines for food, and the animals have little defence against them.

Do they shoot their quills?

There is a well-established story that a porcupine will shoot its quills at an enemy, and many zoologists have been at pains to explain that this is nonsense. The best explanation given so far comes from the American naturalist, William J Long, when writing of the North American porcupine, which we shall be dealing with under tree porcupine. He has described how one night he rolled rocks towards a porcupine on the ground to see how it would react. He saw the porcupine flick its tail in a sidewise blow, and later he found quills that were broken in hitting the rock. He also tells of a woodsman trying to tame a porcupine. In the morning he used to find quills outside the wire-netting of the cage; evidence perhaps of a roving dog having startled the porcupine. In these and other instances Long quotes he assumes that the porcupine's natural reaction to an intruder is to flick its tail sharply, throwing off loose quills.

Although these explanations for an old story come from the New World, the story itself originated in the Old World and was probably first associated with the crested porcupine. It is of interest that the story as it is usually told today is of the porcupine deliberately shooting its quills. We cannot blame our forefathers for this because if we turn to the 15th-century natural history book, the *Hortus Sanitatis*, we read merely that the porcupine 'looses its spines from its back'. The rest has been added later. For example, in Churchill's *Voyages* (1744) we read 'if they are vexed they can by contracting themselves cast [their quills] forth with such strength that they kill man or beast'.

Cuddly companion

The brushtailed porcupines look smaller than the crested porcupines largely because their quills are shorter. Their tails are, however, longer, with a tuft of quills at the end. A story from Sierra Leone tells of a young pet brushtailed porcupine, hand-reared and allowed the run of the bungalow. It had been given a piece of soft cloth in the corner of a room. It seemed content for a few days, then became restless and uneasy. In due course it found its way to the bathroom, discovered the lavatory brush, with bristles almost as stout as its own quills, took this to its sleeping place and nestled beside it, content. Was it missing its mother?

En garde: sensing danger, a cornered porcupine raises its spines. In dealing with attacks, the 'killer punch' of the porcupine is the accurate, sideways slap of its spine-armoured tail.

Jane Burton: Photo Res

class	**Mammalia**
order	**Rodentia**
family	**Hystricidae**
genera & species	*Hystrix cristata* *Atherurus africanus* others

Cricket

There are 1 000 species of cricket, found throughout the world except in polar regions. Apart from the mole crickets, of which there are two species, one in Europe and another in North America, the various kinds differ only slightly. The smallest members are wingless, $\frac{1}{5}$ in. long, and they live in ants' nests, feeding on the ants' oil secretions. These crickets are found only in parts of the northern hemisphere.

Typical crickets resemble grasshoppers and locusts and also the bush crickets, sometimes called long-horned grasshoppers or, in America, katydids. All have long hindlegs used for jumping. Crickets differ from grasshoppers, but resemble bush crickets, in having long, thread-like antennae. They produce sound in the same way as bush crickets and, like them, have hearing organs, or 'ears', in the form of a pit on each front leg. Crickets hold their wings flat over the back with the edges sharply bent down at the sides, and there is a pair of jointed appendages, or cerci, at the tip of the abdomen. The female carries a stiff tubular ovipositor through which the eggs are laid. Most crickets are black or brown in colour.

Crickets for all situations

The house cricket has been spread all over the world by man but is probably a native of North Africa and southwest Asia. In temperate climates it can live only indoors or in rotting refuse heaps which give continual warmth. It is brown, a little over $\frac{1}{2}$ in. long, has fully developed wings and long, angled hindlegs. It hides by day and comes out at night to look for scraps of food, when the males make their small chirping song to attract females. The field cricket, once common in southern England but now rare, ranges across Europe to North Africa. Nearly 1 in. long, shiny black with pale yellow markings at the bases of the forewings, it has a large head, compared with the body. The hindwings are so reduced that field crickets cannot fly. They live on heaths, preferring warm south-facing slopes. The adults hibernate in burrows dug with their large powerful jaws. The wood cricket, small and brown, less than $\frac{1}{2}$ in. long, ranges across the southern half of Europe, into western Asia and North Africa. It is found sparingly in a few southern English counties. It has no hindwings and cannot fly.

The mole cricket, once common, but now very rare in Britain, is found all over Europe, western Asia and North Africa. Dark brown and covered with a fine velvety hair, it is $1\frac{1}{2}$ in. long and lacks the long jumping hindlegs of a typical cricket. Its forelegs are modified for digging, and in action they look much like the forelegs of a mole. The hindwings are fully developed and mole crickets fly about freely.

The scaly cricket of the Mediterranean area seems to be found at only one point in the British Isles, at Chesil Beach, Dorset.

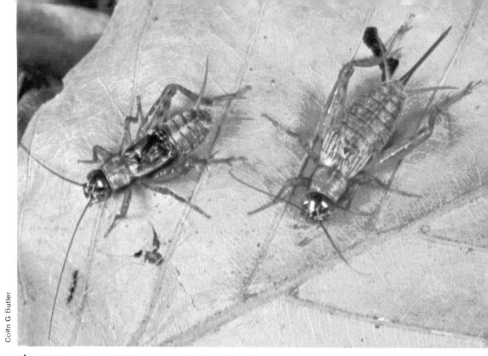

Coln G Butler

△ Adult wood crickets (female at right). Female crickets are distinguished by their long ovipositor.
▽ Female tree cricket: this is one of the bush crickets or long-horned grasshoppers. The ovipositor of the bush cricket is sabre-like and curves upward. In true crickets it is straight and lance-like.

Keystone

Colin G Butler

△ *The heavy-bodied, short-winged mole cricket has powerful front legs, well equipped for digging, and armed with cutting edges for dealing with rootlets. It drives long, shallow tunnels just below the surface — and despite its subterranean tastes it is a perfectly capable flier.*

This has probably been introduced from ships calling at Portland Harbour.

Eat almost anything

Crickets are mainly vegetarian but will take insect food, the proportion varying not only with the species but with circumstances. They will eat dead animal food as well as household scraps. This omnivorous diet has made it easy for the house cricket to live alongside man, and it has given, falsely, a bad reputation to the mole cricket. This is often regarded as a pest and it can sometimes do damage to root crops, but for the most part it feeds on insects.

Calling for mates

The sound of the cricket, once welcome, tends today to be regarded as a nuisance. It is produced by stridulation, rubbing the finely toothed vein on the right forewing against the hind edge of the left forewing. A clear area on the left wing acts as a resonator. The male sits at the mouth of his burrow singing while the female wanders about, guided by his song, until she finds him. Female crickets become excited after they hear the song of a male through a telephone, showing that it is to this song and not to scent or sight of the male that they react.

The male cricket deposits his sperm in small capsules, known as spermatophores, which are taken up by the female.

The field cricket lays her eggs during the summer by inserting them into the ground with her ovipositor. The young hatch fully grown the following spring, after hiber-

▽ *The sound mechanism of the cricket*
It is produced by the rapid friction of the cricket's wings — like a man rubbing his hands together. The finely-toothed file vein on the underside of the right forewing is rubbed against the scraper on the hind edge of the left forewing. The bottom illustration shows the overlapping action of the wings during the cricket's song. This song is, in every sense of the word, a love song. Experiments have shown that it is the song — not the scent or the sight of the male — which excites the female cricket.

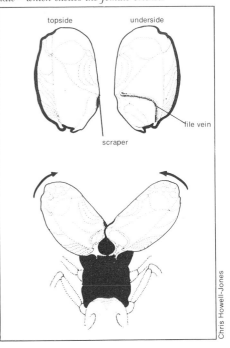

topside   underside

file vein

scraper

Chris Howell-Jones

705

NA Callow: NHPA

△ *Superb camouflage: the sharply-jointed legs of a bush cricket in the field blend perfectly with the angles of the surrounding vegetation.*

▽ *The startling colour of a bush cricket's face. Unlike grasshoppers, crickets and bush crickets have long, thread-like sensitive antennae.*

PH Ward

nation. The adults die in July and August. The wood cricket lays her eggs in autumn, the young hatching the following spring and hibernating to complete their growth in the second summer. Consequently adults of one year can never meet adults of the year immediately past or following. This has led to 'even-year' and 'odd-year' wood crickets which seem to be different races biologically isolated from each other.

The mole cricket lays her eggs in spring in an underground nest and remains with them for up to 2 weeks until they hatch.

The thermometer cricket

The American tree crickets of the genus *Oecanthus* are very sensitive to temperature when singing. The rate of the chirps is speeded up as the temperature rises so exactly that the temperature in degrees Fahrenheit can be calculated quite accurately by timing them. You tell the temperature by counting the number of chirps in 15 seconds and adding 39. If you have a thermometer and no watch, the cricket can be used as a timer: just multiply the temperature by 4 and subtract 160 to find the number of chirps uttered per minute.

Chinese cricket matches

The Chinese have long had an interest in and sympathy for insects, which is reflected in their art. Crickets especially fascinated them by their singing and their pugnacity. Many varieties have been selectively bred for their musical qualities, and others have been specially bred for fighting. Both were kept in small bamboo cages.

The points looked for in a fighting cricket were loud chirping, big head, long legs, and broad backs. Successful fighters were pampered pets fed on special foods including a soup made from a special flower and mosquitoes gorged with blood from their owner's arm. But they were starved before a fight to step up their fighting spirit.

Fights were staged in special bowls on tables with silk covers. A referee recited the past deeds of the contestants before encouraging them to fight by prodding them with a fine hair. Bets were laid and the end usually came when one cricket bit off the other's head, to earn the victor an entry in letters of gold on an ivory scroll, as *shou lip* (conquering cricket).

At first cricket fighting was the costly pastime of the leisurely scholar of Imperial times. Later it became an entertainment of less literate people. Even 40 years ago the 'sport' had degenerated to little better than an amusing old custom, rapidly dying out. Today it is played only by children.

phylum	**Arthropoda**
class	**Insecta**
order	**Orthoptera**
family	**Gryllidae**
genera & species	***Acheta domesticus*** *house cricket* ***Gryllus campestris*** *field cricket* ***Nemobius sylvestris*** *wood cricket* ***Gryllotalpa gryllotalpa*** *mole cricket* *others*

Yellowfin croakers. Apart from their extraordinary capacity for sound output, croakers are fairly ordinary carnivorous fishes with almost-touching twin dorsal fins.

Croaker

Croaker is the name given to nearly 200 species of the family of North American fishes, remarkable for the noises they make. Some of them have been called drums or drum-fishes. They usually have a rounded snout, a single dorsal fin, the front part being spiny. Some have a number of small barbels under the chin. Most of them are used as food-fishes. One, known as tutova **Cynosion macdonaldi,** *of the Gulf of California, may weigh 220 lbs, although most of them weigh only a few pounds.*

The Atlantic croaker is well known from Massachusetts to Argentina. These are fairly ordinary carnivorous fishes laying small eggs which, since each contains an oil globule, float at the surface.

Submarine choristers

By far the most spectacular feature of these fishes is the way in which their noises are used like bird song. They are not the only fishes to do this, but as a family they are outstanding in their performances. The sounds are made in most instances by the vibration of muscles with the swimbladder acting as resonator. Sometimes the muscles are attached directly to the surface of the swimbladder, in other species the muscles are attached to the body wall. In all the use is similar: by contraction and relaxation, at a rate of about 24 contractions a second, the muscle is made to vibrate almost like the strings of a guitar. The sounds have been variously described as drumming, humming, purring, whistling, creaking, croaking, hissing, snorting, even a 'melodious vocal effort'. In some the sounds are relatively feeble, but the loudest of the croakers has been heard by a person, 6 ft above the surface of the sea on the deck of a boat, while the fish was calling from a depth of nearly 60 ft. In Malaya fishermen locate the fish by their sounds.

Fishes not deaf

It used to be argued that fishes are unable to hear, just as it used to be supposed they made no sounds. Fishes in which the swimbladder is not directly connected to the bones of the inner ear can respond to frequencies between 13 and 2 000–3 000 cycles per second. Where there is a connection they can respond to frequencies between 16 and 10 000 cps. The noises they make are well within these ranges, but are mainly low notes.

The sounds are put to many uses in different species of fishes: to enable members of a shoal to keep in touch, possibly as an echo-sounder for depth, for breeding and as an expression of emotions. Illustrating the last of these we have the experience in a public aquarium in the United States. Visitors could, by pressing a button, hear yellowfin and spotfin croakers 'talking' in one of the tanks. All went well until the fishes had settled in and felt at home, when they ceased being loquacious—and visitors had to be content with a recording.

Million-strong choir

The evidence for the other uses is equally scanty and this study is as yet in its infancy. As to members of a shoal keeping in touch, we have observations of the kind recorded for croakers living in the seas around Japan. These are known to assemble in large schools of up to a million and synchronize their drumming. In many species of croakers the volume of sound given out increases as the breeding season approaches, reaches a peak during it, and dies out afterwards. In a few species the sounds begin in the evening, reaching a high pitch towards midnight then sharply dying away. It has been shown by close observation that some species have a dawn chorus, others have both dawn and dusk choruses. In some species only the males 'croak', in others both sexes do so. All this is so like what is found in birds that it seems reasonable the croakers are using their 'guitars' for the same purposes.

Some croakers lack a swimbladder and, as if not wishing to be outdone by their relatives, they make a small amount of sound by grinding their teeth.

The Unsilent Sea

There was a time when we thought of the dark depths as being noiseless and talked of 'The Silent Sea'. With the development of underwater listening devices, this notion has been blown skyhigh. In addition to the croakers and the many other fishes now known to break the underwater silence, it has been discovered that whales, dolphins and porpoises are always chattering to each other or using sounds to test the depth of water beneath them, or to locate food. Even lowly shrimps and prawns add to the submarine cacophony.

There are other sounds to add to the confusion. A submarine in the First World War followed a supposed enemy submarine, only to find it was picking up the heartbeat of a large whale! In the Second World War, with more sophisticated listening devices, submarines, picking up the sounds of croakers and other fishes, suspected enemy craft were in the neighbourhood. Later they used the sound barrage to mask their own noises. It was wartime experiences of this kind that gave a stimulus to research on sound-producing fishes.

The sirens unmasked

Modern naval personnel were not the first to be deceived. It has been suggested that the song of the Sirens, the subject of the Greek myth, may have been nothing more than the 'voices' of the meagre or weakfish, which is common in the Mediterranean. This is a member of the croaker family which ranges from southern Australia to South Africa and the Mediterranean. Occasional individuals, up to 6 ft or more long, appear from time to time off the coasts of the British Isles.

◁ The sound mechanics of a croaker's swimbladder, with the cutaway sections' plan views at far left. At a very rapid rate—about 24 contractions per second—the muscle surrounding the bladder cavities vibrates with much the same effect as the strings of a guitar, with the bladder cavities amplifying the sound.

vagus nerve

muscle

cavity

muscle

muscle

septum

air bladder

gas glands

class	**Osteichthyes**
order	**Perciformes**
family	**Sciaenidae**
genera & species	***Micropogon undulatus*** Atlantic croaker
	Roncador stearnsi spotfin croaker
	Argyrosomus regius meagre
	Umbrina roncador yellowfin croaker
	others

Like an extra for a film on the first amphibious reptiles, a small saltwater crocodile comes ashore in Queensland, Australia. Unlike alligators, crocodiles can be found in brackish waters, estuaries, and swimming out at sea.

Crocodile

*The crocodiles and their close relatives
alligators, caimans and gharials are the
sole survivors of the great group of
reptiles, the Archosauria, that included the
well-known and awe-inspiring dinosaurs.
The crocodile family itself includes the
dwarf crocodiles and the false gharial as
well as the dozen or so species of true
crocodiles.*

*Crocodiles are often distinguished by
the shape of the snout. This is long and
broad in the Nile crocodile, the best-known
species, short in the Indian marsh crocodile or mugger, and long and narrow in
the false gharial. The differences between
crocodiles and alligators are set out under
alligator, p. 67.*

*As with many large, fearsome animals,
the size of crocodiles has been exaggerated.
There is reliable evidence for the Nile
crocodile reaching 20 ft and American and
Orinoco crocodiles have measured 23 ft. At
the other extreme the Congo dwarf crocodile
has never been found to exceed 3 ft 9 in.
Now that crocodiles have been hunted too
intensively, large ones have become
extremely rare.*

Cold-blooded lover of warmth

Crocodiles are found in the warmer parts of
the world, in Africa, Asia, Australia and
America. Unlike alligators, they are often
found in brackish water and sometimes they
even swim out to sea. Estuarine crocodiles
swim between the islands of the Malay
Archipelago and stray ones have been
found in the Fijis and other remote islands.

Reptiles are said to be cold-blooded because they cannot maintain their body
temperatures within fine limits, as can
mammals and birds. A reptile's body temperature is usually within a few degrees of
that of its surroundings. It cannot shiver to
keep warm or sweat to keep cool. Many
reptiles, however, can keep their body temperatures from varying too much by following a daily routine to avoid extremes of
temperature. Crocodiles do this. They come
out of the water at sunrise and lie on the
banks basking in the sun. When their bodies
have warmed up, they either move into the
shade or back into the water, escaping the
full strength of the midday sun. Then in the
late afternoon they bask again, and return
to the water by nightfall. By staying underwater at night they conserve heat, because
water holds its heat better than air.

Stones in their stomachs

When crocodiles come out of the water they
generally stay near the bank, although
occasionally they wander some distance in
search of water, and can cause great conster-
nation by appearing in towns. They are
generally sluggish, but, considering their
bulky bodies and relatively short legs,
they are capable of unexpected bursts
of speed. They have three distinct gaits.
There is a normal walk, with the body
lifted well off the ground with the legs under
the body—a gait most unlike the popular

709

D Paterson: Photo Res

△ A crocodile heads for the water in its normal walking gait: body well clear of the ground, with the legs striding stiffly beneath the body.

▷ The drifting menace—crocodiles in their classic lurking pose, motionless, awash, for all the world like drifting logs.

Jane Burton: Photo Res

△ Young Nile crocodiles bask on a river bank whose soil is polished from the friction of crocodile bellies sliding towards the water.

▽ Crocodiles taking to water in a hurry slide over the edge of river banks on their bellies, using their legs as paddles.

D Paterson: Photo Res

Simon Trevor: Photo Res

△ *Saltwater or estuarine crocodile: one of the world's most dangerous crocodiles, it can reach lengths of over 20 ft.*

▽ *A python falls victim to a hungry crocodile. Once the snake is dead, the crocodile tears off pieces and swallows them whole.*

conception of a crocodile walking. More familiar is the tobogganing used when dashing into the water. The crocodile slides on its belly, using its legs as paddles. The third method is used by a young crocodile which will occasionally gallop along with the front and back legs working together, like a bounding squirrel.

In the water, crocodiles float very low, with little more than eyes and nostrils showing. They habitually carry several pounds of stones in their stomachs, which help to stabilise their bodies. The stones lie in the stomach, below the centre of gravity and work as a counterpoise to the buoyant lungs. This is particularly useful when the crocodiles are fairly young. At that age they are top heavy and cannot float easily at the surface.

Maneaters: myth and fact

For the first year of their lives, young crocodiles feed on small animals, frogs, dragonflies, crabs and even mosquito larvae. Young crocodiles have been seen cornering the larvae by curving their bodies and tails around them. Larger animals are stalked. The baby crocodile swims stealthily towards its prey then pounces, snapping at it with a sideways movement of the jaws, necessary because the crocodile's eyes are at the side of its head.

As a crocodile grows the amount of insects in its diet falls, and it turns to eating snails and fish. The adult crocodiles continue to catch fish but turn increasingly to trapping mammals and birds. They capture their prey by lying in wait near game trails or waterholes. When a victim approaches the crocodile will seize it and drag it underwater or knock it over with a blow from its tail or head. Once the victim is pulled into the water the crocodile has a definite advantage. Drowning soon stills the victim's struggles, and, grasping a limb in its jaws, the crocodile may roll over and over so that the victim is dismembered.

Crocodiles are well-known as maneaters — but how true is this reputation? The maneating habit varies and it may be that only certain individuals will attack man. In parts of Africa, crocodiles are not regarded as a menace at all, while elsewhere palisades have to be erected at the water's edge to allow the women to fetch water in safety. It seems that crocodiles are likely to be more aggressive when their streams and pools dry up so they cannot escape, or when they are guarding their young.

In the crocodile's nest

The Nile crocodile breeds when 5–10 years old. By this time it is 7–10 ft long. The full-grown males stake out their territories along the banks and share them with younger males and females. They defend the territories by fighting, which may sometimes end in one contestant being killed.

A male crocodile approaches a female crocodile and displays to her by thrashing the water with his snout and tail. They swim in circles with the male on the outside trying to get near her so he can put a forelimb over her body and mate.

Up to 90 eggs are laid during the dry season. They hatch 4 months later, during the rainy season when there are plenty of insects about for the babies to feed on.

The Nile crocodile and the marsh crocodile dig pits 2 ft deep for their nests, but the estuarine crocodile of northern Australia and southeast Asia makes a mound of leaves. The nests are built near water and shade, where the female can guard her brood and keep herself cool. During the incubation period she stays by the nest defending it against enemies, including other crocodiles, although in colonies they sometimes nest only a few yards apart.

The baby crocodiles begin to grunt before hatching. This is the signal for the mother to uncover the nest. The babies climb out and the female, sometimes the male also, takes the hatchlings in the mouth to carry them to water. The hatchlings disperse when 6-8 weeks old. Meanwhile they mill about at the water's edge, defended by both parents.

The young Nile crocodiles are about 1 ft long at hatching and for their first 7 years they grow at a rate of about 10 in. a year.

Cannibals

The mother crocodile has to be on her guard all the time as many animals will wait for their chance to eat the eggs or the baby crocodiles. Their main enemy is the monitor lizard. They are bold enough to dig underneath the crocodile as she lies over her nest, and once a male monitor was seen to decoy a crocodile away from the nest while the female stole the eggs. Other crocodiles, herons, mongooses, turtles, eagles and predatory fish all eat baby crocodiles. Adult crocodiles have been killed by lions, elephants, and leopards, and hippopotamuses will attack crocodiles in defence of their young.

Crocodiles are cannibals, so basking groups are always sorted out into parties of equal size and the smaller crocodiles keep well away from the bigger ones.

△ *Hatching out: while still in the egg, baby Nile crocodiles grunt a signal to the mother to uncover the nest.*

▽ *Prelude to feeding: prey trapped in its vice-like jaws, a crocodile returns to the water where it will take its meal at leisure.*

Crocodile tears

If we say that someone is shedding crocodile tears it means that they are showing grief or sympathy that they do not really mean. The idea that crocodiles are hypocrites is an ancient one, and is described in TH White's translation of a 12th century bestiary: 'Crocodiles lie by night in the water, by day on land, because hypocrites, however luxuriously they live by night, delight to be said to live holily and justly by day.' The hypocrisy seems to be manifested in the form of tears, and malicious or misunderstanding comparisons are made with women's tears. Thus when Desdemona weeps, Othello complains:

'O devil, devil!
If that the earth could teem with woman's tears,
Each drop she falls would prove a crocodile.'

John Hawkins explains crocodile's tears as meaning 'that as the Crocodile when he crieth, goeth then about most to deceive, so doth a woman commonly when she weepeth'. The deception practised by the 'cruell craftie crocodile' is that it lures unwary travellers into drawing near to find out what is the matter.

Crocodiles today do have reason to cry. More than half the world's 21 species of crocodile are now endangered. Crocodile skin is made into handbags and shoes, and probably at least half the crocodile skin products on sale in the US were imported illegally, as they are made of species protected in their country of origin. In Thailand, attempts to farm crocodiles for their skins have had some success, which could help save some species.

class	**Reptilia**
order	**Crocodilia**
family	**Crocodylidae**
genera & species	***Crocodylus niloticus*** *Nile crocodile*
	C. porosus *estuarine crocodile*
	C. palustris *marsh crocodile*
	Osteolaemus *dwarf crocodiles*
	Tomistoma schlegeli *false gharial*

▷ *'African crocodiles at home': a romanticized print shows waterfowl scattering in panic from the threat of an evil-looking flock of crocodiles. But, as the picture below shows, nearby birds are in no danger when crocodiles haul out onto the bank to bask with jaws agape. Birds can safely pick parasites from the skin of basking crocodiles, and have been seen to pick leeches and food fragments from crocodiles' teeth and tongues. The birds get away with this because basking crocodiles are not interested in hunting—even food in the mouth does not interest them. Indeed, crocodiles have a definite taste for cannibalism, and so basking groups are always made up of crocodiles of equal size. Smaller crocodiles take care to keep well away from the bigger ones.*

714